You Can Date Boys When You're Forty

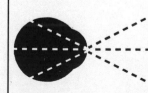
This Large Print Book carries the
Seal of Approval of N.A.V.H.

You Can Date Boys When You're Forty

DAVE BARRY ON PARENTING AND OTHER TOPICS HE KNOWS VERY LITTLE ABOUT

DAVE BARRY

THORNDIKE PRESS
A part of Gale, Cengage Learning

GALE
CENGAGE Learning·

Farmington Hills, Mich • San Francisco • New York • Waterville, Maine
Meriden, Conn • Mason, Ohio • Chicago

GALE
CENGAGE Learning®

LIBRARY OF CONGRESS CATALOGING-IN-PUBLICATION DATA

Barry, Dave.
  You Can Date Boys When You're Forty : Dave Barry on Parenting and
Other Topics He Knows Very Little About / by Dave Barry.
    pages cm (Thorndike press large print core)
    ISBN 978-1-4104-6537-5 (hardback) — ISBN 1-4104-6537-3 (hardcover)
    1. Family—Humor. 2. Parenting—Humor. 3. Large type books. I. Title.
  PN6231.F3B375 2014b
  306.85'0207—dc23   2014000843

Published in 2014 by arrangement with G. P. Putnam's Sons, a member
of Penguin Group (USA) LLC, a Penguin Random House Company

Printed in the United States of America
1 2 3 4 5 6 7 18 17 16 15 14

To my children, Rob and Sophie,
who, against all odds, turned out sane

CONTENTS

■ ■ ■ ■

INTRODUCTION

■ ■ ■ ■

This is not really a book about parenting. I say this because the title clearly refers to parenting, which may have given you the impression that the actual *book* is about parenting. But there's a wise old saying that goes: "You can't judge a book by its cover." Like so many wise old sayings, this is stupid, because of course most of the time you *can* judge a book by its cover. The whole *point* of the cover is to tell you what the book is about. For example, if the cover says *Cooking on a Budget,* you know the book contains inexpensive recipes; and if the cover says *Lose Weight Fast,* you know the book contains lies.

But as I say, this book isn't about parenting. It *mentions* parenting, but it also covers many other topics, including grammar, sex, camels, women, brain surgery, sex with women, how to become a professional author, airlines, Justin Bieber and death.

That's why my original idea was to give the book a more vague and general title. Here are some of the titles I submitted to the publisher:

Dave Barry's Vague General Book of Humor Topics

Dave Barry's Guide to Whatever This Book Is

About Dave Barry: A Dave Barry Book, by Dave Barry

Dave Barry: You Probably Thought He Was Dead

But the marketing people wanted something more specific, and they liked the idea of a title that was about family and/or parenting. So after rejecting several more of my suggestions (including *Without Family, We Would Have Nothing, Except Way More Money and Spare Time*) they went with the current title, *You Can Date Boys When You're Forty.*

Those words do appear in one of the essays in this book, and they are words that I have actually said to my daughter, Sophie. As I write this, Sophie is thirteen years old, which, as you veteran parents of daughters know, is a terrifying age because of puberty. Girls do not go through puberty the way boys do. For boys, puberty is a gradual process — it took me decades — and it's not all that drastic. When the boy is done undergoing puberty, he's hairier and smellier, but still basically the same.

Female puberty is a whole different kettle of biological fish. For years my daughter was this sweet, innocent little girl who played with dolls, slept with stuffed animals and viewed me as a wise authority figure because of all the amazing things I knew how to do, such as tell time. Then one day at about 4:30 in the afternoon, Sophie went into her bathroom (which is pink) and, *WHOOM,* some kind of massive hormone bomb went off in there. She emerged maybe forty-five minutes later having aged, biologically, at least seven years. Suddenly she was this *woman,* with legs and everything, walking around. The same thing happened pretty much simultaneously to her friends — all of them were suddenly beautiful, feminine, poised, sophisticated and several linear feet taller than the boys their age.

The day the hormone bomb detonated marked the end of the era wherein my daughter viewed me as an authority. These days, pretty much the only time she turns to me for guidance is when she can't find the Cinnamon Toast Crunch. When she needs to discuss anything more important — school, relationships, hair, clothes, makeup, hair accessories and biological matters I don't even want to think about — she confers with her several hundred closest girlfriends or my wife, who is also a woman. I am *way* out of the loop. I don't even know where the loop *is.*

Nevertheless, I am, legally, Sophie's father, and I have certain fundamental obligations, the main one being to protect her from harm, with "harm" defined as "men." As a lifelong male myself, I am well aware of the way we think, and I don't want anybody thinking things like that within a thousand-yard radius of my daughter.

The problem I am facing right now is boys, which, biologically, are nothing more than short men. My daughter's school is infested with them. Lately they have taken to hanging around our house, darting around out there on bicycles and skateboards and trying to act as though they are not thinking about what they are thinking about, which we all know is *exactly* what they are thinking about.

Here's what really bothers me: *Sometimes*

14

they get inside the house.

I blame my wife. If it were up to me, our house would be surrounded by giant (but humane) traps baited with some kind of bait that would be attractive to thirteen-year-old boys, such as fireworks or shorts that are even baggier than the shorts they're already wearing. Every now and then we'd hear the loud *THWONK* of a steel door slamming shut, indicating that a thirteen-year-old boy had come too close to the house. I would then go outside and, after a stern warning, drive the boy out to the Everglades and release him into the wild.

But my wife allows them to come in. She has never been a thirteen-year-old boy, so she thinks it's OK if sometimes one of them watches TV with Sophie, the two of them eating popcorn and sitting in the family room *on the exact same sofa.* If it were up to me, I would insist that the boy had to sit on an entirely separate piece of furniture, which would be located in Iceland. But because of my wife's naive soft-heartedness we have this potentially catastrophic situation that requires me to casually stroll past the family room every eight to ten seconds, back and forth and back and forth, a dad on patrol, each time casually glancing inside to make sure Nothing Is Happening. I'm

15

thinking of getting some kind of firearm, which every now and then I would casually discharge into the family-room ceiling. Haha! THAT will give Mr. Short Man something to think about!

Only twenty-seven more years to go.

But I have drifted away from my point, which is that this is not really a book about parenting. It's about many things, which you will find out if I ever stop introducing it so you can go ahead and read it. I hope you enjoy it, and I hope that, amid the laughs, you find some actual nuggets of wisdom. If you do, let me know what they are, OK? I'll be hovering right outside the family room.

SOPHIE, STELLA AND THE BIEBER PLAN

In the movie *Taken,* Liam Neeson plays a father whose daughter is kidnapped by evil pervert sex traffickers with foreign accents. Fortunately, Liam's character is a former spy, and he uses his espionage skills to go on a desperate quest, during which he terminates an estimated 125 bad guys with his bare hands before he finally tracks down his daughter and saves her.

Taken is on cable a lot, and every time I stumble across it I watch the whole thing because it combines two artistic themes with classic enduring appeal:

Liam Neeson beating the crap out of foreign perverts, and
Fatherhood.

If you're a man with a daughter, you can't watch this movie without imagining yourself in Liam's position — wondering how far *you* would go for the sake of your daughter, what desperate life-threatening measures you would be willing to take.

Well, I don't have to wonder anymore. I know exactly what I would do because I have already made the ultimate sacrifice: I took my daughter to a Justin Bieber concert.

How bad was it? you ask.

It was so bad that I cannot hear you asking me how bad it was. My hearing has been destroyed by seventeen thousand puberty-crazed girls shrieking at the decibel level of global thermonuclear war. It turns out that the noise teenage girls make to express rapturous happiness is the same noise they would make if their feet were being gnawed off by badgers. Also, for some reason being happy makes them cry: The girl next to me spent the entire concert bawling and screaming, quote, "I LOVE YOU!" directly into my right ear.

She was not screaming to me of course. She was screaming to cute-boy Canadian heartthrob Justin Bieber, as were all the other girls, including my daughter Sophie and her BFF,* Stella Sable. Sophie and

* "BFF" stands for "Best Friends Forever." This is a term that girls my daughter's age use to describe essentially everyone they know.

Stella wore matching purple tutus (purple, as you are no doubt aware, is Justin's favorite color) and spent the entire concert bouncing up and down, shrieking and vibrating like tuning forks. They are *big* fans. Sophie has covered one corner of her room — she calls it the Corner of Appreciation — with pictures of Justin Bieber gazing at the camera with the soulful expression of a person who truly believes, deep in his heart, that he is the best-looking human ever. On March 1 (which, as you are no doubt aware, is Justin Bieber's birthday) Sophie posted on Instagram* that he is, quote, "the perfectest person on the planet."

One day, while I was looking at the Corner of Appreciation, Sophie and I had the following exchange:

Me: You know, Justin Bieber doesn't have any idea who you are.
Sophie: Not *yet.*

This exchange disturbed me. I don't want my daughter's life goal to be to meet (and I say this respectfully) an over-hyped twerp.

* Instagram is an Internet service that young people use to post photographs of themselves every eight minutes so their BFFs will not forget what they look like.

Don't get me wrong: I'm not one of those fathers who think no man will ever be good enough for their daughters. I'm sure there's somebody out there who is worthy of Sophie, and I sincerely hope that she meets him someday, with "someday" defined as "after I have been dead for a minimum of three months and all efforts to revive me have failed." Even then, if Sophie is going to go on dates with this male, I want to go along. My body can ride in the backseat, with an air freshener.

Speaking of death: My wife nearly experienced it before the concert started. I have seen my wife perform some amazing physical feats; I once saw her produce, from somewhere inside her body, *a live human being.* But nothing I've seen her do was as brave, if not foolhardy, as what she did when we got to the Justin Bieber concert; namely, she purchased officially licensed Justin Bieber merchandise for Sophie and Stella. To do this, she had to battle her way through what was basically a mom riot — several hundred frenzied women* engaged in a desperate elbow-throwing struggle against other moms to reach the merchandise

* There were roughly eight men at the Justin Bieber concert, counting the janitorial staff.

counter so they could pay upwards of fifty dollars apiece for Justin Bieber T-shirts for their daughters.

God forbid this should happen, but: If we ever go to war with Japan again, and they embed their forces deep inside heavily fortified caves on Iwo Jima again, instead of sending in the Marines, all we need to do is put the word around that the Japanese forces are in possession of overpriced Justin Bieber merchandise. Within minutes they will be overrun by moms fully capable of decapitating an opposing shopper using only their MasterCards.

The concert itself was also pretty brutal, lasting (this is an estimate) twenty-seven hours. We had to stand the whole time because everybody else stood the whole time because that is how excited everybody was. Justin Bieber was preceded by two lesser heartthrobs. You could tell they ranked below Justin because they had fewer backup dancers. Your modern singing star does not go to the bathroom without backup dancers. Your modern musical concert consists of the singer prancing from one side of the stage to the other accompanied by a clot of dancers, everybody frantically performing synchronized dance moves and pelvic thrusts, looking like people having sex with invisible partners while being pursued by bees. At times the dancing looks silly, but it serves a vital artistic function; namely, keeping you from noticing that the music (and I say this respectfully) sucks.

OK, perhaps "sucks" is too strong a word.* Perhaps I am just being a flatulent old fossil clinging to memories of the Golden Age of Rock 'n' Roll, back when I was young and all four Beatles were alive and nobody I knew had ever heard of gum disease. Musical acts in those days didn't have to distract you with dancers because, goldarnit, they had *talent.* When you went to see, for example, Sly and the Family Stone, you did not go expecting to see dance routines. You went expecting to see a funktastic band made up of highly entertaining musical performers who, in all probability, were not going to show up.

Headline acts that failed to appear were a distinguishing feature of the Golden Age of Rock 'n' Roll. Back then, the concertgoing experience often consisted of sitting in an auditorium amid dense clouds of smoke, listening to some nervous promoter announce, for the eighth time in three hours, that the headline act was *at that very mo-*

* Not really! The music sucks.

24

ment en route to the venue, when, in fact, the headline act was passed out facedown in a puddle of vomit in an entirely different time zone.

But my point is that during the G. A. of R. and R., on those occasions when the headline acts *did* show up, they didn't race all over the stage inside a clot of hyperactive backup dancers. They stayed in one place, which made them easy to keep track of, which was helpful if you had spent some time inside the smoke cloud, if you know what I mean. Here's an example of what I mean: In approximately 1969, I attended a performance by Jesse Colin Young and the Youngbloods at the Electric Factory in Philadelphia, and I was able to watch the entire show lying on my back on the floor next to the stage pretty much directly underneath one of the Youngbloods, who was known as "Banana." I did get stepped on occasionally, but overall I had a relaxed, mellow experience as well as an excellent view of the band, which stayed in one place the whole night and never attempted any dance maneuvers, and which for all I know is still standing in basically the same spot at the Electric Factory.

If I had lain on the floor at the Justin Bieber concert, within seconds I would have been trampled into human lasagna. I had to stay on my feet in the throbbing, screaming crowd, which shrieked even louder whenever Justin and his backup dancers pranced past, or when Justin did something especially awesome, such as remove his sunglasses. The most exciting moment, which caused a level of shriekage that I'm sure alarmed dogs as far away as Canada, came when Justin took off his shirt and revealed his physique, which reminded me (and I say this respectfully) of the Geico Gecko.

But as thrilling as that was, it was not the highlight of the concert. The highlight, for me at least, came toward the end, when Sophie and Stella decided to execute their plan to invite Justin Bieber to their bat mitzvahs.* They had both brought large square white envelopes containing official invitations: On Stella's envelope, she had written, "Justin please come to my bat mitzvah ♡." Sophie's envelope said "I ♡ you! Please come to my Bat Mitzvah!" Their plan was to somehow get the invitations to Justin Bie-

* A bat mitzvah (for boys, it's *bar* mitzvah) is a Jewish religious ceremony in which a thirteen-year-old child formally becomes a thirteen-year-old child who has received a lot of gift checks from relatives he or she does not always know.

26

ber, who would read them and decide to attend their bat mitzvahs.

Sophie and Stella spent the entire concert clutching their envelopes, vibrating and shrieking and watching the Bieber/dancer clot prance back and forth. But they couldn't get near the stage because the crowd was too thick. Finally, as Justin Bieber went into his last song, they realized that their opportunity was slipping away. They shouted something to my wife and me — I couldn't hear a word — then they turned and plunged into the crowd, lost from our view. A minute later, the dancer clot came prancing back in our direction. The mob of shrieking fans surged forward, and for just an instant, through an opening in the mass of heads in front of me, I got a clear view of Justin Bieber. In that same instant, I saw two large square white envelopes arc through the air and into the spotlight, then flutter to the stage near his feet.

Guess what happened next.

If you guessed that, against all odds, Justin Bieber glanced down and, somehow, amid all the dancing and shrieking, noticed these two adorable purple-tutu-clad girls in the crowd, then suddenly stopped — that's right, *stopped,* right in the middle of the song — and then, with a winning smile and a wink to Sophie and Stella that was easily the greatest thrill of their young lives, reached down, picked up the bat mitzvah invitations and *stuck them into his pocket,* then you are (and I say this respectfully) an idiot. Rock-star pants don't even *have* working pockets. Bieber and the clot pranced right on past, leaving the envelopes lying on the stage.

I assume Bieber never saw the invitations. I know he didn't come to Sophie's bat mitzvah party. Which was his loss because it was a fine event, except for a terrifying few seconds when I was hoisted into the air on a chair being thrust wildly up and down* by a group of men who had consumed so much tequila that they could easily have launched me out a window without noticing it until they put the chair down empty. ("Hey! Where's Dave?" "Dave who?")

But other than that, the party was wonderful. The best part, for me, was the last dance of the night, the Father-Daughter Dance. That's when I got to hold Sophie in my

* Having out-of-shape middle-aged men who have been drinking carry people around in chairs is another ancient Jewish tradition, originated by ancient Jewish orthopedic surgeons.

28

arms, gaze into her smiling face and marvel at the fact that my daughter — who five minutes ago was a little red poop factory I carried around like a football — had somehow transformed into this radiant, beautiful, poised young woman, getting ready to go out in the world and break many hearts.

She'll probably have her own heart broken a few times, too. But she'll do just fine out there in the world, Sophie will, I'm sure of that, because she's a strong, sensible and self-confident person. Also, if any man even *starts* to treat her wrong, I will summon my inner Liam Neeson and wreak vengeance upon that man, even if I am eighty-six years old and have to use a weaponized walker. Because she's a special girl.

And Justin, if you're reading this: You had your chance.

Postscript

Since I wrote this essay, things have changed between Sophie and Justin. She no longer thinks he's the perfectest person on the planet. In fact, she now thinks he's kind of a jerk, and she has uninstalled the Corner of Appreciation. I'd be thrilled about this, except that the place in Sophie's heart formerly occupied by Justin has been taken over by a boy band called One Direction. There are five of them.

■ ■ ■ ■

MANLINESS

■ ■ ■ ■

We live in ridiculously convenient times. Think about it: Whenever you need any kind of information, about *anything,* day or night, no matter where you are, you can just tap your finger on your "smart" phone and within seconds an answer will appear, as if by magic, on the screen. Granted, this answer will be wrong because it comes from the Internet, which is infested with teen-agers, lunatics and Anthony Weiner. But it's *convenient.*

Today everything is convenient. You cook your meals by pushing a microwave button. Your car shifts itself, and your GPS tells you where to go. If you go to a men's public restroom, you don't even have to flush the urinal! This tedious chore is a thing of the past because the urinal now has a small electronic "eye" connected to the Central Restroom Command Post, located deep underground somewhere near Omaha,

Nebraska, where highly trained workers watch you on high-definition TV screens and make the flush decision for you. ("I say we push the button." "Not yet! He's still shaking it!" "He should have those red spots looked at.")

And then there's travel. A century ago, it took a week to get from New York to California; today you can board a plane at La-Guardia and six hours later — think about that: *six hours later*! — you will, as if by magic, still be sitting in the plane at La-Guardia because "LaGuardia" is Italian for "You will never actually take off." But during those six hours you can be highly productive by using your "smart" phone to get on the Internet.

So we have it pretty easy. But we have paid a price for all this convenience: *We don't know how to do anything anymore.* We're helpless without our technology. Have you ever been standing in line to pay a cashier when something went wrong with the electronic cash register? Suddenly your safe, comfortable, modern world crumbles and you are plunged into a terrifying nightmare postapocalyptic hell where people might have to do math USING ONLY THEIR BRAINS.

Regular adult Americans are no more

capable of doing math than they are of photosynthesis. If you hand a cashier a twenty-dollar bill for an item costing $13.47, both you and the cashier are going to look at the cash register to see how much you get back and both of you will unquestioningly accept the cash register's decision. It may say $6.53; it may say $5.89; it may be in a generous mood and say $8.41. But whatever it says, that's how much change you will get because both you and the cashier know the machine is WAY smarter than you.

A while back, my daughter asked me to help her with her math homework, which involved doing long division without a calculator. There was a time, somewhere around 1963, when I definitely knew how to do long division; I figured this knowledge was still lying around in my brain somewhere. I mean, I can remember many other things from 1963. That was the year when the Beach Boys came out with their album *Surfer Girl,* and I can recall every word from every track on it, including an obscure and genuinely idiotic song called "Our Car Club," which contains, among other lyrics, these:

We'll get the roughest and the toughest

35

initiation we can find
And if you want to try to get in, we'll really
    put you through the grind
'Cause THIS club's the VERY BEST!

I haven't heard "Car Club" for decades, but I typed those lyrics without looking them up. My brain stashed them away in a safe place, in case I would need them someday in a lyrics-related emergency. My brain did not, however, elect to save the instructions for doing long division. So when I tried to help my daughter, I was useless. I had a vague recollection that you start by dividing the littler number (or maybe just part of the littler number) into just the *first* part of the bigger number, then you multiply something and then you put the result down below. But I wasn't sure *where* down below, exactly, you put the result, and I had no idea what you did with it after that. 'Cause THIS club's the VERY BEST!

I tried for several painful minutes to show my daughter how to do long division, at which point she gently told me I should go back to watching *Storage Wars* and she would figure out long division on her own. And she did. I don't know where she got the information. Probably from the Internet. Possibly even from Anthony Weiner.

But it's not my inability to do long division that really bothers me. What really bothers me is that, like many modern American men, I don't know how to do anything *manly* anymore. And by "manly," I do not mean "physical." A lot of us do physical things, but these are yuppie fitness things like "spinning," and "crunches," and working on our "core," and running half marathons and then putting "13.1" stickers on our hybrid cars so everybody will know what total cardiovascular badasses we are.

That's not manly. I'll tell you who was manly: the early American pioneers. Those guys didn't even know they *had* cores. But they definitely had large manhoods. They set out into the vast untracked wilderness with nothing but a musket and a sack of hardtack and hominy, and they had to survive out there for months, even years, completely on their own, sleeping on the ground in bear-infested forests. That's why they brought the hardtack: to throw at the bears. They had no idea why they brought hominy. Like you, they had no idea what "hominy" means. It sounds like some kind of disease.

Patient: What is it, doc?
Doctor: I'm afraid you have the hominy.

Patient: Not the hominy!

But the point is, these pioneering men did not do "crunches." These men *crunched the damn continent* — blazing trails, fording rivers, crossing mountain ranges, building log cabins, forging things with forges, etc. We modern men can't do *any* of those things. We don't have the vaguest idea how to ford a river. We'd check our phones to see if we had a fording app and, if not, we'd give up, go back home and work on our cores.

What happened? How did American men get transformed from masculine, self-reliant doers into Teletubbies with abs? I think we can place the blame for this — as well as almost every other bad thing, including disco, "light" beer and Donald Trump — on the Baby Boomers. We grew up soft. Our parents had the Great Depression; we had Captain Kangaroo. They were the Greatest Generation; we are Generation Wuss.

I know for a fact that my father was way manlier than I am. He was not a particularly large, muscular, hairy or masculine-looking individual; he was a bald, nearsighted, mild-mannered Presbyterian minister. But here's one thing he did, and I am not making this up: *He built our house.* Yes. He couldn't afford to hire a builder, so he did it himself.

He cleared the land by hand, dug the footings with a pick and shovel, poured the foundation, framed the house, nailed the roof on, installed the plumbing and electrical wiring, hung the Sheetrock, installed the windows, doors and floors, and so on. My earliest childhood memories are of my dad working on our house evenings and weekends, wearing a diaper tied around his head to keep the sweat out of his eyes. It took him years to finish. But when he was done, guess what? *We had a pretty crappy house.*

No, that's harsh. Our house did have problems, though. It was drafty and it leaked, and often the only way to get the plumbing to work (this became one of my chores) was to go outside and climb down into the "pump house" — a dank, dark hole that was home to seventy-eight percent of the Earth's spider population — and prime the pump by manually blowing air into a disgusting, slime-covered thing until Mom yelled from the kitchen that the water was back on.

So it was not a perfect house. But it *was* a house, and my father, who had no training in construction, built it pretty much single-handedly. It was not until years later, when I became a homeowner capable of causing several thousand dollars' worth of damage by attempting a simple toilet repair, that I really appreciated the magnitude of my father's achievement. There's no way I could do anything that remotely approached it. My father had a utility room filled with serious tools — winches, axes, sledgehammers, a variety of drills and power saws, even an adze, which is a very manly tool, although it, too, sounds like a disease. ("If we don't treat that hominy, it could develop into full-blown adze.")

Here's what my homeowner tool collection consists of: duct tape, a smallish hammer and 283,000 tiny random pieces of hardware for hanging pictures. Hanging pictures is my only real manual skill. If we have a global nuclear war and civilization is wiped out and I happen to be one of the small band of surviving humans, I will not be a big help.

First Survivor: I'll forage for edible roots.
Second Survivor: I'll look for water.
Third Survivor: I'll build a shelter from fallen trees.
Me: And I'll hang pictures!
First Survivor: We'll eat him first.

The scary thing is, the wussification of

American men is getting worse. Pathetic as we Boomer males are, we're Daniel Boone compared with the generations that have come after us. Forget about fording rivers; these kids today can't move out of their parents' houses! They're twenty-eight years old and their mom is still doing their laundry! And this "rap" music they listen to! You call that music? I call that shouting! Why, back in my day, we had *real* musicians, bands like the Beach Boys, who . . . Wait a minute! Who pooped in my drawers?

<END GEEZER MODE>

But getting back to the issue at hand: We American men have lost our national manhood and I say it's time we got it back. We need to learn to do the kinds of manly things our forefathers knew how to do. To get us started, I've created a list of some basic skills that every man should have, along with instructions. You may rest assured that these instructions are correct. I got them from the Internet.

THINGS A MAN SHOULD KNOW HOW TO DO

How to Cook a Steak on the Grill

1. Make sure you choose a good steak.

41

The main "cuts" of steak are the Brisket, the Loin, the Round, the Chuck, the Rump, the Groin, the Niblick, the Flanker, the Grommet, the Cosine and the Stirrup. They are all basically the same because they all come from the inside of a cow. You should select a manly looking steak that is approximately the size and density of a standard manhole cover and does not have too many visible fly eggs.

2. Many people like to enhance the flavor of the steak by soaking it ahead of time in marinade or rubbing it with a blend of herbs and spices.

3. These people are pansies.

4. Place the steak horizontally on the grill oriented along an east-west axis.

5. Drink a timing beer. (VERY IMPORTANT: Not a "light" beer.)

6. When the beer is done, check the steak by prodding it firmly yet gen-

tly with your right forefinger. If it feels cold, you need to light the grill. (This should have been Step 1.)

7. Drink another timing beer.

8. Turn the steak over, using barbecue tongs or a No. 2 profilated Phillips screwdriver with a ten-inch titanium-coated shank.

9. Drink another timing beer.

10. Check the steak to determine how done it is, using this chart:

DONENESS OF STEAK	COLOR OF STEAK
Rare	Brown
Medium Rare	Brown
Medium	Brown
Medium Well	Brown
Well	Brown

11. If the steak is covered with molten or flaming plastic, you failed to remove it from the packaging. (This should also have been Step 1.)

12. Spray the steak with a fire extin-
    guisher if necessary and serve it
    outdoors in a dark area.

13. This might be a good time to switch
    to tequila.

How to Survive If You Are Lost in a Forest and Night Is Falling

1. Always remember that the most
   important rule of wilderness survival is: *Do not panic.*

2. Granted, there are probably dangerous wild carnivorous animals lurking nearby.

3. Wolverines, for example.

4. According to Wikipedia, "The wol-
   verine has a reputation for ferocity
   and strength out of proportion to
   its size, with the documented ability
   to kill prey many times larger than
   itself."

5. And do not get Wikipedia started
   on the question of venomous
   snakes.

44

6. But you *must not panic.*

7. FOR THE LOVE OF GOD, GET A GRIP ON YOURSELF.

8. Gather flammable wood to make a fire. The best kind of wood in this situation is the "fire log," which is easy to identify because it comes in a box of six.

9. Check your pockets to see if you have matches or a cigarette lighter, which of course you will not. You would not dream of smoking cigarettes because you are a modern, crunch-doing, health-conscious, risk-averse individual.

10. A fat lot of good that's doing you now with the wolverines closing in.

11. Fortunately, there are other ways to start a fire. Position yourself over your fire log and, with a quick motion of your wrist, strike a piece of flint against a piece of steel to make a spark.

12. Just kidding! If you had flint and

steel, you would not be the kind of nimrod who gets lost in the forest in the first place.

13. An old Indian trick is to rub two sticks together rapidly to create friction.

14. This method has never once, in human history, resulted in an actual fire.

15. It's just one of those things that Indians enjoy tricking white people into doing.

16. Other examples are canoeing, face painting and "hominy."

17. Since there will be no fire, your only hope of surviving is to stay up all night making noises that will keep animals away. Most leading wilderness survival experts recommend that you sing the "Macarena," which goes as follows:

Something something something
   something something something
   something something,

Something something something
　something something something
　something something,
Something something something
　something something something
　something something,
Hey Macarena!

18. You should also do the hand motions because carnivorous animals can see in the dark. You may feel silly, but consider: Not one single person has been killed in the wilderness by animals while doing the "Macarena" since the National Forest Service began keeping records on this in 1902.

19. If you are still alive in the morning, carefully note the direction in which the sun rises. This will be either east or west, depending on what hemisphere you are in. Using this information, you can determine which way north and south are and, from there, you can calculate the time of day to within roughly two hours.

20. Another option is to look at your watch.

21. Carefully scan the horizon, noting landmarks — a river, a hill, a valley, a Motel 6 sign, etc. Use these to create a "mental map" of your current position.

22. Keeping all of this information in mind, calmly, and without panicking, run in a random direction, throwing your hands into the air and shouting, "I DON'T WANT TO DIE!"

23. If you are anywhere in North America, within twenty minutes you will come to a Starbucks.

24. There, you can purchase emergency scones while the staff calls for help.

How to Sail a Sailboat

1. Figure out where you want to go.

2. Whichever way it is, do NOT aim the sailboat in that direction.

3. Aim the sailboat in some *other* direction.

4. Trust me, this is the way sailboaters do it.

5. They are heavy drinkers.

How to Dress

1. Get hold of the Sunday *New York Times.*

2. Turn to the Men's Fashion section and make note of what it says the Modern Man is wearing.

3. Whatever it is, *do not wear it.*

4. EVER.

5. Exhibit A is "capri pants."

6. A man should not wear capri pants.

7. This is not a matter of "taste" or "style." This is a matter of *scientific fact.*

8. A man who puts on capri pants, no matter how suave and attractive he is otherwise, immediately transforms himself into a Category 5

douche.

9. Yes, there are foreign countries where many men wear capri pants.

10. *None of these countries has ever won a war.*

11. Yet for decades now, the *Times* has been trying to get American men to wear capri pants.

12. I don't know why the *Times* does this.

13. It just seems to have a men's capri pants bee in its bonnet.

14. Or perhaps the men's capri pants industry has obtained photographs of the *Times* men's fashion editor in a compromising situation with an underage Shetland pony.

15. But whatever the reason, every six months or so, the *Times* declares that capri pants are the "Hot New Trend for the Modern Man."

16. Of course the vast majority of

American men are not stupid enough to fall for this.

17. Tragically, however, there are a pathetic, desperately insecure few who do.

18. We call these people New Yorkers.

19. Another example is scarves.

20. There are times when a man *should* wear a scarf.

21. For example, if he is competing in the Iditarod.

22. But a man should never wear a scarf in warm weather, or indoors.

23. Nevertheless, several years ago — we assume the *Times* was also behind this — thousands of New York men suddenly started sporting long, flowing scarves everywhere they went, including probably the shower.

24. It was like a mass audition for *Lawrence of Arabia*.

25. Fortunately, the Scarf Trend ended, although it was followed by the Hipster Ironic Fedora Trend, which was actually worse.

26. As a general rule, do not wear "ironic" clothing unless you wish to make the bold fashion statement: "I'm still living off my parents."

27. Also, be aware that there is an appropriate time to wear a tank top and that time is not when you are in a restaurant or airport.

28. People do not go to those places in hopes of catching a glimpse of your armpits.

29. Finally, never wear any designer clothing on which the designer logo is taller than the actual designer.

30. I am looking at you, Ralph Lauren.

How to Order a Bottle of Wine in a Restaurant

1. Look at the wine list and tell the waiter which wine you want.

2. When the waiter brings it to you, take a sip.

3. If it's OK, say it's OK.

4. Then shut up about the wine.

5. Don't talk about the wine anymore.

6. *Nobody gives a shit how much you know about wine, OK?*

7. And, for God's sake, don't keep holding your glass up and sloshing the wine around and looking at it as if it's magical unicorn blood.

8. It's *wine,* for God's sake.

9. In an hour it will be urine, same as Bud Light.

How to Jump-start Your Car When the Battery Is Dead

1. Obtain a working car from somewhere and park it next to your car.

2. Or, if the owner isn't around, you

could just take off in the working car.

3. No, that would be wrong.

4. On both cars, locate the hood, which is a big flat piece of metal in the front with bird poop on it.

5. Open both hoods. There will be a button or lever inside the car on the driver's side that you need to push or pull, and then a latch somewhere under the front of the hood that you need to reach in and release. So your best bet is to use a crowbar.

6. Locate your car's battery. It will be a black box partly covered with a whitish-greenish fuzz. This is car leprosy. *Do not touch it.*

7. Obtain some jumper cables from somewhere.

8. Call 911 and let them know there might be an emergency soon.

9. Do this next part VERY, VERY

CAREFULLY OR YOU WILL DIE.

10. Connect one end of the *red* jumper cable to the *positive* terminal (also called the ignition or carburetor) on your car's battery. Then connect the other end of the red cable to an electronic part such as the radio of the opposing car. Repeat this process *in the opposite order* with the *black* jumper cable, taking care to reverse the polarity.

11. Try to start your car. If the engine explodes in a giant fireball, something is wrong.

12. Maybe you should have somebody else try to start your car while you go get coffee a minimum of 150 yards away.

13. If by some miracle your car actually starts, *do not turn it off ever again.*

14. When you drive, be alert for further signs of trouble such as a flickering of your headlights, which is an indication of a problem in your

electrical system; or a collision with a building, which is an indication that you forgot to put the hood back down.

How to Ride a Horse

1. Always approach the horse from the southwest at an eighty-degree angle, bearing in mind that the horse hates you, and with good reason, because it knows you intend to sit on it.

2. The horse would like nothing more than to kick you in the head and then poop all over your unconscious body.

3. Establish dominance by making eye contact with the horse. This is not a figure of speech: You should literally press your eyeballs against the horse's eyeballs. This lets the horse know that you are just as crazy as it is.

4. Mount the horse by firmly grasping the fetlock, inserting your foot deep into the bridle and, with a thrusting motion, raising yourself until your

thighs are straddling the horse's loin quarters.

5. At this point, it is perfectly normal for both of you to be sexually aroused.

6. The way you get the horse to start moving depends on whether you are riding "English" or "Western" style:

English style: Gently flick the reins.
Western style: Discharge your sidearm into the air.

7. Steer the horse by tugging on the reins, which are attached to its mouth. This signals to the horse that you enjoy inflicting pain on it.

8. Note that in English-style riding, a *left* tug will turn the horse *right.*

9. Keep riding the horse until you think it is too tired to bite you, then stop it by steering it into a hedge, or, if you're riding Western style, a saloon.

10. To get off the horse, give the com-

mand "Kneel!" If the horse fails to obey, you will have to stay up there until help arrives with a ladder.

11. Western riders may use their side-arms to signal distress.

How to Perform Emergency First Aid

1. Making a conscious effort not to whimper, evaluate the overall situation. Is anybody actually hurt? If nobody is, you probably do not need to perform emergency first aid, although for legal reasons it does not hurt to slap on a few tourniquets just in case.

2. If there is a victim, determine whether he or she is conscious by singing a few bars of the Barry Manilow classic "Copacabana." If the victim is conscious, he or she will try to hit you.

3. Keep the victim calm by administering several brisk facial slaps and shouting, "CALM DOWN, DAMMIT! DO YOU WANT TO DIE??"

4. Very Important: Before attempting any treatment, find out whether the victim has insurance or is planning to pay with cash.

5. Determine what specifically is wrong with the victim by looking for medical symptoms such as paleness (which can indicate hominy), dilated pupils, shortness of breath, a knife handle sticking out of the victim's eye socket or a major limb such as a leg lying detached more than fifteen feet away from the remainder of the victim.

6. Check for fractures by giving all of the victim's remaining limbs a hearty yank. The victim will let you know which limb is fractured.

7. Whatever the problem appears to be, apply direct pressure. Everybody agrees on this.

8. Also remember the "ABC" rule of first aid:
A
Bone
Coming out through the skin is

very bad.

9. If the victim appears to be woozy or "out of it," you will need to perform immediate brain surgery. Every second counts, so *do not wait for the paramedics.* Using a sterilized surgical saw or clean sharpish rock, carefully cut around the circumference of the victim's head just above the ear line and lift it off the top of the skull to expose the brain. When you see what the problem is, apply direct pressure to it.

10. If the victim is feeling bloated, use a six-foot length of bamboo to administer a field enema.

11. To induce vomiting, force the victim to watch an episode of *Here Comes Honey Boo Boo.*

12. Often you can lure a tapeworm out of the victim by placing tapeworm treats* on the ground in the vicinity of the victim's butt, then loudly making statements such as, "We'll

* Always carry some.

just leave these treats here un-
guarded!"

13. If the victim is choking, the most
likely cause is either something
blocking the victim's airway, or an
alien creature about to burst out
from the victim's chest. Whatever
you do, *do not let it get into the
escape shuttle.*

14. When the ambulance arrives, ask
the paramedics if you can operate
the siren.

15. Be sure to apply direct pressure.

WHAT WOMEN WANT

So I read *Fifty Shades of Grey.* This is the book written by female British author "E. L. James" that became a huge bestseller, devoured by pretty much every woman on Earth except my wife (or so she claims).

I think I might be the only man who read this book. I did it sneakily, hiding the cover, especially when I was on an airplane, which actually is a good place to read this book because you have access to a barf bag. I say this because of the writing style, which is . . . OK, here's one tiny sample of the writing style:

"Did you give him our address?"

"No, but stalking is one of his specialties," I muse matter-of-factly.

Kate's brow knits further.

That's right: This is the kind of a book where, instead of saying things, characters muse them, and they are somehow able to muse them *matter-of-factly.* And these matter-of-fact musings cause other characters' brows — which of course were already knitted — to knit still *further.* The book is over five hundred pages long and the whole thing is written like that. If Jane Austen (another bestselling female British author) came back to life and read this book, she would kill herself.

So why did I read it? I read it because, as a man with decades of experience in the field of not knowing what the hell women are thinking, I was hoping this book would give me some answers. Because a lot of women LOVED this book. And they didn't just read it; they responded to it by developing erotic feelings — feelings so powerful that in some cases *they wanted to have sex with their own husbands.*

I know that sounds like crazy talk, but I have firsthand confirmation of this phenomenon from my friend Ron, who is married to my wife's cousin Sonia, a woman. Ron states: "While Sonia was reading the book, I was getting more action than Wilt Chamberlain."

Another friend of mine whose name I will

keep confidential out of respect for his privacy* told me, "I'd be lying on the bed watching *SportsCenter,* and she'd be reading that book and suddenly, *WHOA.*"

So what kind of book is *Fifty Shades of Grey*? I would describe it, literary-genre-wise, as "a porno book." But it's not the kind of porno men are accustomed to. When a man reads porno, he does not want to get bogged down in a bunch of unimportant details about the characters, such as who they are or what they think. A man wants to get right to the porno:

Chapter One

Bart Pronghammer walked into the hotel room and knitted his brow at the sight of a naked woman with breasts like regulation volleyballs.

"Let's have sex," she mused matter-of-factly.

A few paragraphs later they're all done, and the male reader, having invested maybe ninety seconds of his time, can put the book down and go back to watching *SportsCenter.*

Apparently that is not what women want,

* Eddie Friedman.

porno-wise. What women want, to judge from *Fifty Shades of Grey,* is not just people doing It. Many pages go by in this book without any of It getting done, although there is a great deal of thinking and talking about It. The thoughts are provided by the narrator and main character, Anastasia Steele, who is a twenty-one-year-old American woman as well as such a clueless, self-absorbed ninny that you, the reader, find yourself wishing that you still smoked so you would have a cigarette lighter handy and thus could set fire to certain pages, especially the ones where Anastasia is telling you about her "inner goddess." This is a hyperactive imaginary being — I keep picturing Tinker Bell — who reacts in a variety of ways to the many dramatic developments in Anastasia's life, as we see in these actual quotes:

"My inner goddess is swaying and writhing to some primal carnal rhythm."

"My very small inner goddess sways in a gentle victorious samba."

"My inner goddess is doing the Dance of Seven Veils."

"My inner goddess is doing the merengue with some salsa moves."

"My inner goddess has stopped dancing and is staring, too, mouth open and drooling slightly."

"My inner goddess jumps up and down, with cheerleading pom-poms, shouting 'Yes' at me."

"My inner goddess is doing backflips in a routine worthy of a Russian Olympic gymnast."

"My inner goddess pole-vaults over the fifteen-foot bar."

"My inner goddess fist-pumps the air above her chaise longue."

That's right: Her inner goddess, in addition to dancing, cheerleading, pole-vaulting, etc., apparently keeps furniture inside Anastasia's head. Unfortunately, this means there is little room left for Anastasia's brain, which, to judge from her thought process, is about the size of a walnut. On the other hand, Anastasia is physically very attractive, although she never seems to figure this out despite the fact that all the other characters keep telling her, over and over, how darned attractive she is.

As the book begins, Anastasia has somehow managed to complete four years of college, during which time she has had — despite being so physically attractive — no romantic involvement of any kind with anybody. In fact, she's still a virgin. Also, she does not own a computer nor does she know how to operate one. She has no e-mail account, and seems to be only dimly aware of how the Internet works. At one point she says, quote: "Holy cow! I'm on Google!"

That's right, Anastasia uses the expression "Holy cow!" Also, when she gets upset (which is often) she says: "Crap!" When she gets *really* upset, she says: "Double crap!"

In short, Anastasia is a totally believable and realistic depiction of a normal twenty-one-year-old female American college student as she might be imagined by a middle-aged female British author who has lived her entire life in a cave on another planet.

So anyway, early in the book Anastasia meets the main male character, Christian Grey. He is average-looking.

Hah! I am of course joking. He is the handsomest man in the history of men. Lest we forget this crucial fact, Anastasia remarks

70

on Christian's handsomeness at least once every two pages. Her inner goddess repeatedly shits her tiny imaginary leotard over the hotness of this man.

To add to the stark realism of his character, Christian is also, at age twenty-seven, a self-made billionaire. He started a company called, realistically, Grey Enterprises Holdings, Inc., which employs thousands of people engaged in the field of doing some kind of vague business things in accordance with businessy-sounding orders given by Christian over his mobile phone as he stands around in various stylish settings with his worn but stylish jeans hanging loosely off his hips looking unbelievably hot. Christian also is an expert dancer, piano player and glider pilot. Plus he has the ability to read minds and move so fast you can't even see him.

No, sorry, that's Edward from *Twilight*.

So anyway, Anastasia and Christian meet, and he is of course attracted to her, although because of her walnut brain she can't believe this despite the fact that, as I have already noted, *every freaking person she meets* is attracted to her. Christian starts stalking her and pressuring her to engage in — and I do not mean this to sound in any way judgmental — sicko pervert sex. He

71

wants to tie her up with ropes, handcuffs, shackles, tape, etc. He wants to blindfold and gag her. He wants to spank her, whip her, flog her, cane her, paddle her, put nipple *and* genital clamps on her, bite her and use hot wax on her. We know this because *he asks her to sign a contract agreeing to let him do these things to her.* Yes! To be fair, the contract clearly states that there will be "no acts involving fire play . . . urination or defecation and the products thereof" and "no acts involving children or animals." Because that's the kind of old-fashioned cornball romantic Christian is.

What do you think Anastasia does when she sees this contract? Do you think she gets herself a restraining order and an industrial-sized drum of pepper spray, which would be the response of a normal sane woman or reasonably intelligent cocker spaniel? Not our Anastasia! Crap no! She decides to go right ahead and get into a sexual relationship with Christian even though she thinks he is a moody weirdo pervert. (But hot!)

In this relationship, Anastasia keeps trying to get Christian to be a regular huggy-kissy-smoochy boyfriend, but he doesn't want to do that. In fact, he doesn't even want her to *touch* him because he has a Dark Secret in his past. What he wants to do, and keeps trying to get Anastasia to let him do, is tie her up and flog her with various implements, as per the contract. She doesn't want that, but she keeps seeing Christian anyway because she finds him so darned fascinating, in the sense of hot.

So the plot is: They have sex, she wants to smooch, he wants to flog, there's a bunch of talking about this, they have sex again, she again wants to smooch, he again wants to flog, there's a bunch more talking about this, and so on for several hundred word-filled pages.

Finally, Anastasia decides to let Christian flog her, to see what it would be like. So he takes a belt and flogs her on the butt. Then, in the dramatic climax to the story, the moment we have been building up to, Anastasia comes to a shocking, life-changing realization, which nobody could have foreseen in a million years: *Getting flogged on the butt hurts*. Yes! It's painful! Anastasia does not like it! Double crap!!

So she breaks up with him.

And then . . .

And then the book is over.

I'm serious. That's the plot.

There are two more books in this series, titled *Fifty Shades Darker* and *The Third Fifty Shades Book That Was Required to Make It a*

Trilogy. I assume these books bring these two lovebirds back together, as well as revealing the Dark Secret in Christian's past. I don't know because I haven't read them, although I fully intend to do so in the future if the only alternative is crucifixion.

But never mind the other two books. The first book was the big one, the one tens of millions of women could not put down. So to get back to my original question, from the standpoint of a guy sincerely trying to understand women: Why was this book so incredibly popular? When so many women get so emotionally involved in a badly written, comically unrealistic porno yarn, what does this tell us? That women are basically insane? Yes.

I mean no! No. Of course it does not tell us that. What it tells us is this: *Women are interested in sex.*

This may be obvious to women, but, trust me, it is not obvious to men. In fact, it is contrary to everything men are led to believe, dating back to puberty. When a young man goes through puberty, he basically turns into a walking boner. He would happily have sex with any receptive female or room-temperature vegetable.* He thinks

* Don't think this doesn't happen.

about having sex *all the time,* but the only person he knows who wants to have sex with him is himself. He would be very interested in having sex with an actual human female, but he has no earthly idea how to accomplish this. Generally he spends *years* in this frustrating state before he manages to find a woman willing to have sex with him. Some males become so desperate that they resort to paying for sex, or even running for Congress.

As a result of these experiences, men come to believe — and this belief is reinforced throughout their dating lives as they get shot down more often than the Egyptian Air Force — that women are nowhere *near* as interested in sex as they are; that women are capable, somehow, of not thinking about sex *for entire minutes at a time.*

So men exist in a state of perpetual confusion about when, exactly, human females are receptive to the idea of having sex. Men wish that women had some kind of clear signaling mechanism, as is found in other species. Dogs, for example. Years ago I had a female German shepherd puppy named Shawna. For the first few months of her existence, she exhibited no interest whatsoever in having sex with male dogs, and the male dogs in the neighborhood exhibited no particular interest in her.

And then one spring day, *BAM,* Shawna became a woman. To get the word out, she turned into a 50,000-watt AM hormone transmitter, broadcasting a scent that traveled vast distances at the speed of lust. Horny male dogs were showing up from as far away as New Zealand. The house was surrounded, day and night. You didn't dare to open the door for fear that a furry canine sex missile would burst past you and commence humping. There were no misunderstandings between the genders; nobody was being subtle. The male dogs were, like, "I gather from the odor you are emitting that you are receptive to having sex with a male!" And Shawna was, like, "That is correct! I very much desire to be mounted from the rear 'doggie-style' and I do not care by whom!"

This went on for several tense days. And then, *BAM,* Shawna was over it. She stopped broadcasting and the males disappeared, and shortly thereafter Shawna was fixed and she never heard from the male dogs again, not even a postcard.

Unfortunately, human sexuality does not work this way, except on *Jersey Shore.* Human females are less obvious, which means human males must be able to pick up subtle cues, and unfortunately we are terrible at this. So we tend to assume that women just aren't that interested.

This is why the immense popularity of *Fifty Shades of Grey* is actually great news for men. It's a signal from the female gender — not unlike the one broadcast by Shawna — transmitting an exciting and encouraging message to men everywhere: "We *are* interested in sex! We're just not interested in sex with *you* unless you're a superhot billionaire."

OK, so this is not a *totally* positive message for us men. But we can work with it! We can interpret it to mean that women would like their sex lives to be more interesting. Maybe they wish that we would be more obsessive and stalkerish. Maybe they even secretly fantasize about engaging in unconventional, even "kinky," sexual activities. There is only one way to find out, men: You need to have an honest, "no holds barred" conversation about sex with the special woman in your life. I did this with my wife, and as difficult as this was for me, I'm glad I did because it was very revealing. Here's the complete transcript:

Me: Hey, do you secretly want me to tie you up and flog you?

My wife: No.

Yes, communication is the key to a successful relationship. That, and not peeing in the shower. That's pretty much all the advice I have for you men. In a word: *Be sensitive.* And now, if you'll excuse me, my inner god needs to turn on the TV and watch huge men knock each other down.

■ ■ ■ ■

DEATH

■ ■ ■ ■

I hate my mail.

There was a time when I liked getting mail. I'm talking maybe twenty years ago — a simple, primitive time when you could not even shoot and edit high-definition video with your phone. In those days my mail consisted largely of letters from actual human beings who genuinely cared about me. Granted, most of these people were Ed McMahon. Ed wrote at least four times a week with exciting personal news. "Dear David," Ed would begin because we were on a first-name basis. "You may already have won $17 million!"

Mind you, I never actually *won* seventeen million dollars, but the point is that Ed cared enough about me, as a fellow human, to let me know that I already *might* have. I knew he sincerely cared because his letters always had a picture of his jovial face, beaming out at me with an expression that said

81

"It's ten-thirty a.m. and I've already consumed a fifth of scotch!"

I also used to occasionally receive letters from friends and relatives, usually handwritten, which, for you younger readers, is a kind of writing that you do on paper holding a writing thing in your bare hand. But times have changed. Ed went to that Big *Tonight Show* Couch in the Sky, and most of the rest of us don't send letters anymore. Many younger people have *never* sent a letter. When my son, Rob, was in college, he had to send a letter for some reason that I don't remember. What I do remember is that he called me to ask some technical questions, such as (I am not making any of these questions up):

- Where could he get a stamp?

- Were there different kinds of stamps?

- Well then, which one should he buy?

- How much would it cost?

- What should he physically do with the letter when it was finally ready to go?

Rob was quite annoyed that the letter-mailing procedure was so *complicated.* He felt about it pretty much the way I feel about doing my taxes. Which is why Generation Text doesn't send letters, and, as I say, everyone else has pretty much stopped, too. Which means that all you get in the mail these days is bills and big wads of advertising crap that you immediately throw away. Whenever I read one of those stories about a mail carrier who, instead of delivering the mail, has been putting it in dumpsters, I think: *Why can't* MY *mail carrier do that?*

But it's not the fact that my mail is basically home-delivery landfill that makes me hate it. What makes me hate it is that it reminds me, over and over, six days a week except on federal holidays, that I am old. "Dear David," my mail is saying, "You may already be dead!"

For example, I recently received a letter that begins as follows:

We need your help. We are conducting a survey to determine the interest and needs of those in our community who prefer or would like to know about cremation.

The letter — which comes from a concerned cremation provider in my community — goes on to ask my views about cremation, and whether my loved ones know about my views on cremation, and what I would like my loved ones to do with my ashes (which the letter calls my cremated remains) and — prepare to be surprised — whether I would like to receive "free, no obligation" information on cremation services.

Let me start by saying I am all for cremation. We Barrys are a crematin' clan. Both of my parents, in accordance with their wishes, were cremated. And they weren't even dead yet! (*Rim shot.*)

But seriously: Cremation always seemed to me to be the best post-death option. It's definitely better than being embalmed. I have been to a number of funerals where the deceased had been embalmed and the casket was left open for viewing. What you're *supposed* to think in this situation of course is: *Oh! He or she looks so lifelike!* But the truth is, the deceased never looks lifelike. The deceased always looks like a corpse, which is the last thing you want to see at a funeral.

So I'd rather be a box of ashes, which also has the advantage of being portable. When my dad died, our family — my mom, my sister, my brothers and I — drove his ashes to the cemetery, carried them to the grave and buried them ourselves. We dug the hole, put the ashes in, covered them up, said some stuff, then just stood there for a while, remembering Dad. It was sweet, dignified and unpretentious, like him. As we walked away, my mom was holding on to my arm, both of us weeping. We reached another grave, where Mom stopped and read the name on the gravestone aloud. Then she said: "So *that's* why we don't see him around anymore." Then we walked on, but now we were weeping *and* laughing.

(I mention this so you'll know that my mom had a dark sense of humor and would not have been offended by the cremation joke I made several paragraphs earlier.)

Another good thing about cremation is you can do a lot of different things with the ashes: keep them on the mantel, drop them out of planes, take them to the movies, use them in pranks, etc. One of the best memorial ceremonies I ever attended was in remembrance of Jeff MacNelly, the great cartoonist, and equally great guy, who died of lymphoma at age fifty-two because (if you want my opinion) there is no God. Jeff's sense of humor was not unlike my mom's. I called him up right after he was diagnosed and he said, in his big, booming voice,

"People keep telling me, 'If you have to have cancer, this is the kind to get!' So I guess I should be thrilled." In every conversation I had with Jeff, even when things got bad, he made jokes. There was a lot of laughter at his funeral. Also, drinking.

Jeff loved boats, and he loved Key West. So a few months after he died, a bunch of people who loved Jeff boarded a sailboat in Key West and went out into the ocean, where Jeff's ashes were fired out of a cannon into the sea, after which there was additional drinking. It was great. Jeff would have loved it. The only way he would have loved it more is if the cannon had been aimed at a lawyer.

So ashes give you a lot of post-death options. Whereas in corpse form, you are limited. You can't fire a corpse out of a cannon, as far as I know. Although I would love to be proved wrong.

So I am all for cremation. My point — which you have completely forgotten, and I don't blame you — is that I don't want to get *mail* about it. I don't want to be nagged by cremation companies to think about my cremation options *right now*. I'd much rather think about my cremation options after I'm dead, when I don't have to think about them, if you know what I mean.*

But that's the kind of mail I get these days. I get mail aimed at old people because I am officially an old person. My mail never lets me forget this. I get three or four letters every day just from companies that want to tell me about my Medicare options. Here's the thing: *I don't want to know about my Medicare options.* I don't even want to even think about Medicare because Medicare involves (follow me closely) medical care, which involves medical professionals inserting unnatural objects deep into your personal orifices and always (if you are an old person) discovering that you need Additional Tests. If there was a Medicare option whereby the professionals would be prohibited from coming any closer to you than fifteen feet unless they could see blood spurting from both of your ears, THEN I would be interested in reading about my Medicare options.

I'm looking at one of the Medicare letters right now. Here's how it begins:

65 IS THE NEW 50. AND BEST OF ALL, YOU ARE NOW ELIGIBLE TO JOIN A GREAT HEALTH

* I, personally, do not know what I mean.

CARE PLAN . . .

OK, number one: "BEST OF ALL"? *BEST OF ALL??* You're telling me that the BEST THING about reaching this age is that I'm eligible to join your health care plan? What's the *second*-best thing? Nose hair?

Number two: *Sixty-five is not the new fifty.* Whoever wrote those words is (1) an idiot and (2) not sixty-five. I am sixty-five and I remember being fifty, and they are not remotely the same thing. I'll tell you what sixty-five is: It's *sixty freaking five.* It is an age that is viewed, correctly, throughout the human world, as OLD. If you're sixty-five and you keel over* and die, people don't think: *What a completely unexpected shock!* They think: *Well, he was sixty-five.*

Every day I get the newspaper (which, for you younger readers, is a paper with news written on it) and I check the obituaries to see how many of that day's deceased were younger than I am. That gives me one number, which we will call X. Then I check the People page to see how many of the people who qualify as People and who have birthdays that day — indicating that they

* This is not a figure of speech: By age sixty-five, you have developed an actual keel.

are still alive — are older than I am. This gives me another number, which we will also call X, because at our age we have trouble remembering things. If the first X is smaller than the second X, then it was a good morning of newspaper reading. But most of the time, the first X is bigger. Sometimes the second X is zero: *Not a single People-worthy birthday person is older than I am.* On those days, I put down the newspaper and slowly chew my soy-based meat-free sausage with the realization that it could, statistically, be my last breakfast ever.

So do NOT try to tell me sixty-five is the new anything, Mr. or Ms. Direct Mail Marketing Douchebag.

I'm not kidding about the forgetfulness. Here's a recent example: Every morning, after I feed (in this order) the tropical fish, the dog and my daughter, I go out and get the newspaper. *Every morning* I have done this, for centuries. So one recent morning I was in the kitchen, and the various pets and offspring were eating breakfast, and I said to my wife, "I'm going out to get the newspaper." My wife gave me a look and said, "You already got the newspaper." She then pointed to the newspaper, which she was reading. It was lying on the kitchen counter, where I had just placed it after bringing it in from outside. So I said, quote, "Ha-ha," indicating that I was not at all alarmed by this minor "brain fart" that in no way meant I was well along on the road to becoming a drooling fossil, doddering around with poop in his undershorts.

Then I poured myself a cup of coffee.

Then — this was *at most* ninety seconds later, I thought to myself, quote: *"Hey, I need to go get the newspaper!"*

So I went to the front door, opened it and stepped outside. It was only then that I remembered that I had just made a fool of myself by declaring to my wife, who was reading the newspaper I had just brought inside, that I was going outside to get the newspaper.

I turned around and I saw that my wife was watching me. This was a tricky moment, a moment when quick thinking was required to establish that I had not morphed into the late Walter Brennan (who, for you younger readers, was an actor who portrayed a fantastically old rural coot on an early sixties TV sitcom called *The Real McCoys**). Here is what the shriveled husk of

* VERY DEPRESSING FACT: When *The Real McCoys* first aired, Walter Brennan was *younger than I am now.*

what was once my brain came up with for me to say as I stood there in the doorway looking at my wife looking at me: "I'm just checking the weather. It's gonna be warm."

This was a statement of spectacular idiocy. We live in South Florida. It has been warm here for five hundred and thirty million consecutive years. Going outside to see if this trend is continuing — especially if you have *just been outside* — is not unlike randomly jumping into the air every few seconds to determine whether gravity is still working.

My wife, to her credit, resisted the urge to say anything, and there are definitely things she could have said. *Have you also pooped your underwear?* is only one example. Later that day, however, out of the blue she said, "You weren't 'checking the weather.' "

"No," I admitted. "I'm going senile."

Then we both laughed. Although not that hard.

Speaking of not that hard: I hate Viagra commercials.

Let me stress that there is no shame in needing Viagra, although I personally do not need it, but if I did need it I would not hesitate to acknowledge this, although, as I believe I mentioned earlier, I do not need it. But the commercials are loathsome. First of all, we are talking about a product intended to enable a man to — and here, in the interest of discretion and professionalism, I will employ medical terminology — get a boner. No question, this is important. Human males *need* to get boners; this is one of their three most critical biological functions, along with farting and second-guessing pass-interference calls.

Unfortunately, the human penis is poorly designed. It is the Windows Vista of mammal penises. Other, better-designed mammals — your raccoons, your gorillas, your moles — have no boner issues because the males have actual bones in their penises. Really. It's called a *baculum* and it's brilliant, whoever thought of it. I have, in my office, for legitimate, tax-deductible journalistic reasons, the penis bone of a walrus, which the Eskimos call an *oosik,* and which I call Walter. It's nearly two feet long. It is *very* impressive. You could easily kill a person with Walter. The mature male walrus is basically packing a billy club in his tallywacker. He is *not* worrying about getting a boner. He is *very* confident in his manhood. This is why you almost never see a male walrus driving a Corvette.

But whoever designed human males failed to include the baculum option, so our

CHECKOUT SLIP
BELMONT COUNTY
DISTRICT LIBRARY
740-633-0314
www.bcdlibrary.org
Date charged: 7/27/2018 15:16
Item ID: 33667004030067
Title: Killing Jesus [large print] : a his
tory

Due: 8/17/2018

Date charged: 7/27/2018 15:23
Item ID: 33667004070113
Title: You can date boys when you're forty
 [large print]

Due: 8/17/2018

****

Library Hours
Mon-Thurs: 9 AM-8 PM
Fri: 9 AM-6 PM
Sat: 10 AM-5 PM
Sun: Closed
****

mechanics are trickier. As we age, many of us (although, as I may have mentioned, not me personally) need help. So Viagra and other erectile drugs are a welcome development.

But here's the thing, and I am about to speak for everyone in the United States who is not some kind of degenerate sicko pervert: When we are watching television, in our family room, with our family, which includes our children, and we have chosen to view what is supposed to be family-appropriate programming, such as a sporting event, *we do not want to be exposed to a sixty-second commercial about getting boners.* We do not want to have to answer questions about boners from our younger, more naive children; and we do not want to have to sit in mortified silence while avoiding eye contact with our older, boner-savvy children. In other words, this is a time when we, as a nation, DO NOT WANT BONERS TO COME UP⋆ AT ALL.

And yet they do. There are boners up all over what is theoretically family viewing time. It is Bone-a-Rama. This is grotesquely inappropriate. It also creates a deeply troubling picture of the physical state of the

⋆ Har.

modern American male. You watch an evening of TV and by the fifteenth erectile dysfunction ad you're thinking: *Can't* anybody *in this nation get it up?* Inevitably, if you're an older guy, you start to wonder: *Could this happen to* me?

You especially wonder this because the guys in the Viagra commercials are always more masculine than you are. For example, there's one Viagra commercial, which I have seen dozens of times, in which a rugged aging cowboy is driving a manly pickup truck towing a horse trailer on a rural road and he gets stuck in the mud out there in the middle of nowhere. Is he daunted? No, he is not. The announcer says: "You've reached the age where you don't back down from a challenge."

For the record, this statement is one hundred percent pure bullshit. It is the *opposite* of true. The older you get, the *more likely* you are to back down from a challenge. If you want scientific proof of this, go to YouTube and search for any variation of the phrase "shoot bottle rocket from ass." This will turn up many videos of people attempting to shoot bottle rockets from their asses. It goes without saying that all of these people are males. But more to the point, they are all *young* males. I have no doubt they were all responding to challenges from their friends. "I dare you to shoot a bottle rocket out of your ass!" their friends said. And, being young males and therefore less intelligent than a bowl of grits, they *responded to the challenge.* And then they went to the ER to be treated for, among other things, scrotal burns.

Here is my challenge to you: Find an older man — any older man — and challenge him to shoot a bottle rocket out of his ass. I guarantee you that he will not hesitate: He will immediately back down. Learning when to back down from challenges is one of the main reasons he got to be an older man, as opposed to dead. His current idea of an acceptable challenge is trying to stay up until 10:30 p.m.

Also, for the record: If an older man has trouble getting a boner, he will not view that as a "challenge," any more than he will view a tapeworm or hemorrhoids as a "challenge." He will view it as "a medical problem."

But getting back to the cowboy in the Viagra commercial: He gets out of his stuck pickup and opens the doors to the horse trailer. The announcer says: "This is the age of knowing how to make things happen. So, why would you let something like erectile dysfunction get in the way?" And, by gum, the cowboy *doesn't* let it get in his way. In the very next scene, there are two horses hitched to the front of the pickup, and the cowboy — thanks to the miracle of Viagra — is having sex with *both* of them.

No, that does not happen. At least not during the commercial. Of course we don't know what happens later when the camera is off; we cannot say for certain how the cowboy expresses his gratitude to the horses for towing his truck. We do know it gets lonely out there.

But my point is, if you're an older man watching TV, you're going to be bombarded with commercials suggesting that there is a nationwide epidemic of noodle dick. You inevitably start to wonder: *Could this condition afflict* me? You also wonder this about all the *other* medical conditions — there seem to be thousands — featured in TV commercials for prescription drugs whose names sound like characters in *The Lord of the Rings,* as we see in this comparison chart:

PRESCRIPTION DRUGS	THE LORD OF THE RINGS CHARACTERS
Crestor	Boromir
Zocor	Saruman
Cymbalta	Denethor
Lyrica	Faramir
Chantix	Galadriel

Every one of these commercials features older people (People like you!) suffering from apparently common medical conditions (Conditions *you* very well could be suffering from!) and needing to take prescription drugs (Drugs *you* should probably be taking! Ask your doctor!) despite the possibility of unpleasant side effects ("Discontinue using Faramir if both of your eyeballs explode").

After an evening of watching TV, I'm pretty sure that, one way or another, I'm going to die within hours, which actually doesn't seem so bad because I have also concluded that, manhood-wise, I will soon decline to the point where I could no more get an erection than bench-press the Lincoln Memorial.

So I hate TV as much as I hate my mail.

I do a lot of math these days. It's Death Math. I'll be waiting to pick my daughter up at middle school and I'll start thinking:

OK, so when she graduates from high school, if I live that long, I'll be seventy. When she graduates from college, if I live that long, I'll be seventy-four. And when she starts dating boys, if I live that long, I'll be . . . Jesus, I'd be ninety-two *years old.*

By way of explanation: My daughter is not allowed to date boys until she's forty. This is the only rule I've laid down for her and I think it's reasonable, based on the known scientific fact that boys — even intelligent, thoughtful, loving, sensitive and caring boys — are scum.

When my daughter can legally commence dating (February 24, 2040), I intend to monitor her closely. I intend to do this even if I am deceased. My last will and testament will contain instructions stating that if my daughter goes anywhere in a car with a male belonging to the opposite sex, the urn containing my ashes shall be placed on the console between the passenger and driver's seats, along with a little placard that says "DON'T MIND ME! YOU KIDS HAVE FUN!" The urn will also have a siren that goes off periodically.

I don't want you to think that all I do, now that I'm old, is sit around and think about death. Not at all! Sometimes I also plan my funeral. Here's how I want it to go:

I. ORGAN PRELUDE: "Let a Man Come In and Do the Popcorn" (James Brown)

II. PALLBEARERS ENTER

There will be eight pallbearers to carry the casket. There will not, however, be an actual casket; the pallbearers will be mimes. They will mime setting a heavy casket down in front of the room and feeling very sad. Then they will mime being trapped inside a glass box. Then they will mime suffocating to death.

III. CLERGYMAN ENTERS

The clergyman will say a few words welcoming everyone to the service. He will then realize he is not wearing pants.

IV. CLERGYMAN EXITS

V. AWKWARD EIGHT-MINUTE PAUSE

Note: The mimes may elect to fill this void by performing additional routines.

If this happens, they are to be shot by Navy SEAL snipers.

VI. CLERGYMAN (A DIFFERENT ONE) ENTERS

The clergyman will say a few words welcoming everyone to the service. He will then speak for fifteen minutes on the benefits of becoming an Amway distributor.

VII. CHOIR SONG

The choir will perform the Howlin' Wolf version of the Willie Dixon song "Wang Dang Doodle." Lyrics will be distributed to the audience, which will be urged to sing along for this part:

We gonna romp and tromp till midnight, we
    gonna fuss and fight till daylight
We gonna pitch a wang dang doodle all
    night long

VIII. EULOGY

I would like my eulogy to be given by a close friend or, if he is available, William Shatner. I will not presume to dictate the contents of the eulogy. My only requests are that it (1) be done entirely in a fake Scottish accent, (2) have a Charades portion, and (3) feature, at some point, the word "poontang."

IX. LUCKY SEAT ANNOUNCEMENT

The audience will be instructed to look under their seats. Under one of them will be a small container of my ashes, which the audience member can take home.

X. LIVE PERFORMANCE OF "CANDLE IN THE WIND" BY ELTON JOHN

If Elton John is unavailable, the organist should again play "Let a Man Come In and Do the Popcorn."

XI. PLEDGE OF ALLEGIANCE

XII. CANDY TOSS

XIII. ORGAN POSTLUDE: "Let a Man Come In and Do the Popcorn"

Of course my funeral could be a ways off. As I write these words, I'm looking at the newspaper and this happens to be a pretty good day — the People section is noting the birthdays of *four* celebrities who are older than I am and yet, incredibly, not dead. Granted, they don't all *look* so great; vultures are clearly visible in their publicity shots.

But the point is, they're still around. And, for now, so am I. I've been granted another day of life and I intend to live it to the fullest. But first I'm going to go outside and get the newspaper.

■ ■ ■ ■

NOTHING! REALLY

■ ■ ■ ■

Every morning my wife and I take our dog, Lucy, on a two-mile run.

OK, "two-mile run" is inaccurate. A better way to describe it would be "several hundred closely spaced urination stops."

Urination is a major component of Lucy's lifestyle. Think about the most wonderful thing you've ever experienced — falling in love, seeing your child being born, going an entire day without hearing the name "Kardashian." Remember the joy you felt? That's the kind of joy Lucy feels *every time she smells another dog's urine.* And since we live in a dog-intensive neighborhood, Lucy is in a state of near-constant rapture.

Each morning we leave the house and trot perhaps four steps when, suddenly, *YANK,* Lucy — a big, strong dog who has the ability to create her own planet-level gravitational field — stops and makes herself roughly as mobile as a convenience store, causing my leash arm to come halfway out of its socket. Lucy's nose hoovers the ground and her tail whips around like a snake on amphetamines, which is her way of signaling the fantastic news: *You will never guess what I have found here: DOG WEE-WEE!! Can you BELIEVE it??* Then she squats to squirt some of her own weewee — she has a 275-gallon bladder — on top of the other dog's weewee. To humans, this behavior may seem pointless, even stupid, but it serves an important biological function: It is how one dog signals to another dog the vital information that both of them contain weewee.

When she's done squirting, Lucy permits us to trot a few more steps, whereupon, incredibly, she discovers *another* place where a dog has urinated and, *YANK,* we must stop again. And so on, for two miles. It is slow going. We make about the same rate of progress as Bill Clinton passing through a roomful of women. If the early American pioneers had taken Lucy along on their wagon trains, everything west of Cleveland would still be untamed wilderness.

So our morning "run" takes quite a while, and during this time Michelle and I have a chance to talk. And when I say "Michelle and I," I mean "Michelle." She does the vast majority of the talking. I'd *like* to contribute to the conversation, but I can never think of anything to say. At that point, Michelle and I have been together for at least twelve straight hours. We had dinner together the night before, watched TV together, slept in the same bed together, woke up together, went through the morning routine together and drove our daughter to school together. If I had anything to say to Michelle, I'd have said it by then. So when we're running, the only potential conversational topics that pop up in my mind are the same ones popping up in Lucy's (*Squirrel!*).

Whereas Michelle, who is a woman, always has many new topics she wants to talk about, and every one of these topics reminds her of *other* things she wants to talk about, and those other things remind her of still *more* things she wants to talk about. She is a nuclear reactor of words. But I'm not complaining and I'll tell you why: I don't want to sleep in the driveway.

No, seriously, I enjoy hearing Michelle talk. She's like my own personal talk radio station, Radio Michelle, always full of interesting news, such as what our daughter Sophie is up to. Michelle knows because she actually talks to Sophie. Whereas I do not. I spend a fair amount of time in the car with Sophie, driving her to and from activities, and we're happy in each other's company, but we don't talk: I listen to sports radio and she exchanges texts and Instagram messages with her fourteen million girlfriends. We don't discuss these things with each other because Sophie doesn't really care if the Dolphins need help at offensive tackle and I don't really care if Girlfriend No. 11,368,421 and Girlfriend No. 5,820,327 are mad at Girlfriend No. 7,009,256 because she (I refer here to Girlfriend No. 7,009,256) said something to some boy in the cafeteria.

But Michelle *does* care about these things so she talks to Sophie all the time, which means that when we're on our run she can fill me in on things about our daughter that I would not otherwise know, such as whether she is happy, what grade she is currently in, whether she has had any major operations, etc.

And it's not just Sophie; Michelle talks to *everybody.* She has many, many friends, and when they call, she can talk with them for hours, even if they already talked earlier that day. I have maybe one percent as many close friends as Michelle, and, being males, they *never* call. This is fine with me because if they *did* call, even if we hadn't talked in fifteen years, we would quickly run out of things to talk about. Within seconds we would be discussing the Dolphins' situation at offensive tackle. By the end of a minute we would be down to awkward silence, and that would be that for another fifteen years. Some of my close friends could easily be deceased; this would not have a serious effect on our relationship.

I don't think I'm abnormal. I think I'm a regular male person, and there are plenty more like me. For example: Some years ago, because I needed something to write a column about, I became an official Notary Public in the state of Florida and performed a wedding. The bride, whose name was Pat, gave me the following account of how the groom, Phil, proposed to her:

"One day he was telling me what needed to get done, and he said we needed to register the boat, get a fishing license and get a marriage license. So I said, 'Wait a minute, what was that again?' And he said, 'Register the boat, get a fishing license and get a marriage license.' So I said, 'Are you serious?' And he said, 'Yeah, we've got to register the boat.' "

Phil, a male, did not feel the need to get all blah-blah-blah about his decision to go ahead and engage in matrimony with Pat.

He'd decided that the time had come for them to get hitched, so he informed Pat of this decision, thoughtfully grouping it with other to-do items requiring proper legal documentation.

Another example: I once ate dinner at a Mexican restaurant with a group of about ten women sportswriters and they got to talking about another woman sportswriter, whom they did not like. When I say "got to talking," I mean they talked about this woman, and nothing else, for *two solid hours.* They explored in great detail the reasons why they didn't like her; they analyzed the various possible causes of her behavior; they agonized over whether their feelings toward her were justified; and on and on and *on.* Finally, they noticed me, sitting quietly at the end of the table behind a forest of Dos Equis bottles, and they asked me if a group of men would ever have this kind of discussion about a person whom everyone in the group disliked. I said a group of men would handle it as follows: The name of the disliked person would come up and somebody would say, "What an asshole." Then everybody would nod, and the conversation would turn to a more fruitful topic, such as the situation at offensive tackle.

I realize that I may sound as if I'm pushing the hackneyed old stereotype that women talk way more than men. So let me clarify something: That is *exactly* what I am doing. Because the stereotype is true. It is a scientific fact that women talk more than men. This was proven in a study done by researchers at the University of Maryland and reported on the Internet, a leading source of information. If I understand this study correctly — and I think we can all agree that this is highly unlikely — it concerned a protein called FOXP2, which is associated with vocalization, and which is found, among other places, in the brains of baby rats. In their study, the researchers found that if you separate mother rats from their babies, they will bite you.

No, seriously, the researchers found that the baby rats whose brains contained higher levels of FOXP2 emitted more distress cries and, as a result, the mother rats retrieved these babies first. I was surprised by this. Not the protein part; the part about the mother rats retrieving their babies. I don't think of rats as being maternal. I think of them as being vermin. I assumed that if you separated a mother rat from her babies, she would just shrug* and resume scurrying

---

* Assuming rats can shrug.

around and spreading the bubonic plague. But no: She's a mom! She retrieves her babies! *Aw.*

Then she eats them.

No, I don't know what she does with them and I frankly don't care because — follow me closely here — they are rats. But the scientific point is that the baby rats with more FOXP2 protein in their brains vocalized more than the ones with less. And here's the thing: It turns out that FOXP2 is also found in the brains of humans, and *female humans have more of it.* So there is your scientific reason why women talk more. We still don't know what causes women to wear shoes that hurt, or fill their homes with reeking decorative candles that provide no more illumination than a lukewarm bagel, or watch *The View,* or put small weird-shaped pillows on beds that already *have* pillows, but we assume some kind of mutant brain proteins are also causing these behaviors.

Anyway, I think both men and women can benefit from the Maryland study — men by understanding that women have a biological tendency to vocalize, and women by understanding that it would not kill them to every once in a while just shut up.

Kidding! I am kidding!

But I do think you women can learn something important from this study, which is this: The next time you become frustrated with your husband or boyfriend because you don't think he's sharing his innermost thoughts and feelings with you, remember: Talking is not as easy for him as it is for you. Men are more suited to taking action, such as opening a beer, or opening a second beer.

You should also consider the fact that men, compared to women, don't *have* all that many innermost thoughts and feelings, and the ones we do have we are not necessarily proud of. Consider the situation of a man and a woman on a first date. I guarantee you they are not thinking the same kinds of things:

What the woman is thinking: *He's physically attractive enough, but what about his personality? Is he intelligent? Does he have a good sense of humor? Does he have good manners? Is he self-centered or is he sincerely interested in me? Is he involved in any other relationships? Is he in good physical shape? Does he drink too much? Use drugs? Is he trustworthy? Does he have a good job? Would he be a good provider? What kind of family does he come from? What are his interests? What about his values? Are*

113

our backgrounds similar enough that we would be compatible? Does he want to have children? What kind of parent would he be? Am I talking too much about myself?

What the man is thinking: *She has a vagina!*

Trust me, that's pretty much all he is thinking. Men have that particular thought *a lot.* And they think it in a totally positive way. But it's not something they can *share.* So when you ask us what we're thinking and we answer, "Nothing," take it as a compliment. We're probably thinking about you! Or at least your vagina. Or *somebody's* vagina. Or the situation at offensive tackle.

The point is, whatever we're thinking, you don't really want to know, OK? This doesn't mean you can't have meaningful conversations with us. It just means you'll have to provide the topics and most of the actual words. But that's OK! We don't mind listening! Really.

As long as we can see the TV.

■ ■ ■ ■

"GRAMMAR"

■ ■ ■ ■

We're becoming a nation of illiterates. Ask any group of businesspeople who read a lot of job applications to name their biggest single complaint, and chances are they'll tell you they've gained weight since college, even though back then they ate pizza and drank beer all the time.

But if you clarify that you are asking them about the job applications, chances are they'll tell you that young people today have terrible writing skills. They don't know the rules of grammar or punctuation, they can't spell, they use tiny, unreadable fonts that look like bacteria and they're always texting each other pictures of their private parts, which is not directly related to their writing skills but, dammit, what is *wrong* with these kids?

Who is to blame for this illiteracy? I think that we in the older generation — the parents who raised these young people —

have to look in the mirror and, painful as it is, face the culprit: a combination of factors, including the Internet, reality television, "hip-hop," global climate change and Starbucks.

But whatever the cause, it's a big problem because writing is a crucial life skill. If you're a recent college graduate and you send a poorly written résumé to potential employers, they're going to throw it straight into the trash. Whereas if your résumé is well written and error free, the odds are very good that they're still going to throw it into the trash, because the job market sucks. But they throw the well-written résumés away a little later. *That's* the group you young people want to strive for.

"But," I hear you whining in unison, "isn't grammar hard and boring?"

No, English grammar is *not* "hard and boring." That is a myth. All you have to do is learn a few simple, logical rules. Once you've mastered those, all you have to do is learn nineteen trillion totally illogical exceptions to the rules because otherwise you will sound like an idiot. So reflecting back on the opening sentence of this paragraph, we see that English grammar is, in fact, hard and boring. We'd better get started!

Step one is to learn:

THE PARTS OF SPEECH

The parts of speech are sometimes called the building blocks of grammar, because most of them are rectangular. The main parts of speech are:

Nouns

A noun is a person, place or thing. For example, consider this sentence:

As far as actors, **Leonardo DiCaprio** *is no Marlon Brando.*

In this example, "Leonardo DiCaprio" is a noun because he is a person whereas "Marlon Brando" is not because he died in 2004.

Exception: Zombies, despite being technically dead, can be nouns when used grammatically in lymphatic phrases, such as:

Help! **Zombies** *is eating my spleen!*

Pronouns

Pronouns are words that stand in for nouns when for some reason you don't want to come right out and say the name of the noun:

- You better not let **you know whom** get a load of that hickey.

- I'm not saying who dropped the air

biscuit during the State of the Union speech, but his *initials are Joe Biden.*

- After seven straight hours on the back of Darnell's Harley, Marge was feeling a little funky *down there.*

Verbs

Verbs are words that describe actions.

- What is all that *ruckus*?

- You are *darned tooting.*

- Don't make me come over there and *open up a can of whupass* on your ass.

- *Dang* it!

- When Vernell found the duck sauce on his Barcalounger, he like to threw a *conniption fit.*

- I would describe those actions as *very unusual.*

Exception: If no actual action takes place, the sentence does not need a verb, as in these examples:

120

- Francine watched the entire 2010 season of *Cake Boss*.

- The pitcher threw a no-hitter.

- The president met with congressional leaders to discuss ways to improve the economy.

Adjectives

Adjectives are words that tell you something about a noun:

- For a person of his stature, **Leonardo DiCaprio has quite a large head.**

- In the 1991 movie Critters 3, Leonardo DiCaprio **plays a young man who locks his mean stepfather in a room with space creatures that eat him.**

- The letters in "Leonardo DiCaprio" **can be rearranged to spell "A ripe raccoon dildo."**

Adverbs

Adverbs are words that end in "ly," such as *personally, frankly, manly* and *ugly*. They are used to form parts of sentences, as follows:

- Four people died from wings-related injuries inflicted during a *family* function at Chuck E. Cheese.

- Bernice put a *doily* over the hamster doots.

- *Holy moly,* there's mice in this lasagna.

Prepositions

Prepositions are words such as *in, of, to, from, around, about, aforementioned* and *yonder.* They introduce prepositional phrases, which are used mainly to write song lyrics:

- I've been *through the desert on a horse with no name.*

- I got passion *in my pants* and I ain't afraid to show it.

- *In-A-Gadda-Da-Vida,* baby, don't you know that I'm loving you.

- She'll be coming *'round the mountain* when she comes. / She'll be coming *'round the mountain* when she comes. / She'll be coming 'round the mountain, she'll be coming *'round the mountain,* / She'll be coming *'round the mountain* when she comes.

- *Round round get around* / I get around / Yeah / Get *around round round* I get around.

- Since you put me down there's been owls pukin' *in my bed.*

- Who put the ram *in the rama lama ding dong*?

Very Important Rule: You must never, ever end a sentence with a preposition. Why? Because *Hitler* ended sentences with prepositions, that's why. So if it appears that your sentence is about to end with one, you need to change it:

WRONG	RIGHT
Where is that odor coming from?	*Where is that odor coming from, God damn it?*
Australia is known as "The Land Down Under."	*Australia is known as "The Land Down Underneath."*
What up?	*What up, home dog?*
Come on over.	*Come on over, God damn it.*

Articles

The articles in English are *a, an, the* and sometimes *why.* Grammatically, articles are used to form permutative interjections, as in these examples:

- Like I give *a* rat's ass.

- What *an* idiot.

- Sam *the* Sham and the Pharaohs.

- *Why,* God damn it?

OK, now that we have mastered the "building blocks," let's see how they go together in the next section, titled:

FORMULATING A CORRECT GRAMMATICAL SENTENCE

Every sentence contains two main parts:

- The *subject,* which is the subject of the sentence, and

- The *predicate,* which is the other main part of the sentence.

Consider This Example:

Lester wondered how come lately whenever he called Francine to find out where she was, she always claimed she was in "yoga class," even though, number one, she did not own a yoga mat that Lester knew of, number two, he was not aware of any yoga classes in the greater Waco area that met at 2:30 a.m., not to mention which, number three, one time when he called her, a man in the background yelled, "Francine, hang up the damn phone and take off the rest of your clothes," although Lester was leery of making a fuss about this in light of the recent situation wherein, the morning after he allegedly attended a Monster Truck rally with his brother Wesley, Francine happened to be rooting around under the front seat of his car and found a brassiere that was not remotely her size.

At first glance this sentence appears to be very complex, but when we break it down into its basic components, we suddenly see how our grammatical "building blocks" work together:

SUBJECT	PREDICATE
Lester	wondered how come lately whenever he called Francine to find out where she was, she always claimed she was in "yoga class," even though, number one, she did not own a yoga mat that Lester knew of, number two, he was not aware of any yoga classes in the greater Waco area that met at 2:30 a.m., not to mention which, number three, one time when he called her, a man in the background yelled, "Francine, hang up the damn phone and take off the rest of your clothes," although Lester was leery of making a fuss about this in light of the recent situation wherein, the morning after he allegedly attended a Monster Truck rally with his brother Wesley, Francine happened to be rooting around under the front seat of his car and found a brassiere that was not remotely her size.

When writing sentences, you should always follow this basic format, which has been the "backbone" of English grammar dating back to the ancient Greeks.

The Kinds of Sentences

There are four kinds of sentences:

- *Declarative:* Call me Ishmael.

- *Interrogative:* Call me, Ishmael?

- *Imperative:* Call me Ishmael or I will punch your face in.

- *Text:* ish r u awake? (Picture of private parts.)

Common Sentence Mistakes to Avoid
"Run-on" Sentences

These are sentences that keep on going past the point where you should have ended them:

I don't think you look fat in those pants any more than usual.

Upon graduating from college with honors I was hired as a sales associate by a major brokerage firm and quickly rose to the position of district manager before a time-traveling flamingo ordered me to kill my supervisor.

Sentence Fragments

Sentence fragments occur when you leave out an important grammatical element that is necessary to fully understand the sentence:

WRONG	RIGHT
Thou shalt not kill.	*Thou shalt not kill unless thou hast an expensive legal defense team.*
We show your flight departing on time.	*We show your flight departing on time, but we are lying.*
I'm afraid the biopsy shows you have cancer.	*I'm afraid the biopsy shows you have cancer. Ha-ha, April fool! You should see the look on your face! But seriously, all kidding aside, it turns out you have leprosy.*

Answers to Common Grammatical Questions

Q. What is the difference between "your" and "you're"?

A. Many people are confused by this

because the two words are so much alike, and these people have the intelligence of corn meal. Grammatically, the difference is that "your" is used in expressions of remunerative culpability:

As the bridegroom your responsible irregardless of whomever physically shot them urinals.

Whereas "you're" is used in connubial imprecations:

You cheating bastard, I hope Jasmine cuts you're pecker off.

Q. When do I use "infer" and when do I use "imply"?

A. These two words are often used interchangeably, but, in fact, they have entirely different meanings, as we see in these examples:

Duane inferred that Clark was packing Nutella in his Speedo.

Duane implied that Clark was packing Nutella in his Speedo.

Q. What is the correct use of "decimated"?

A. It is correctly used in arthropodic phrases, such as:

Tina was totally decimated when she sobered up and realized there was nine legs on her forehead spider tattoo.

Q. What about "affect" and "effect"?

A. You should never use either of these words.

Q. What is the proper use of the expression "moot point"?

A. Its proper use is to defeat your opponent in an argument, as follows:

You: *Abraham Lincoln was our first Jewish president.*
Your Opponent: *Lincoln wasn't Jewish.*
You: *That's a moot point.*
Your Opponent: *Very well then, I*

concede.

Q. When should I use "it's" and when should I use "its"?

A. This depends on whether you plan to use an apostrophe somewhere else. Under international grammar rules, there can only be one apostrophe per sentence, as we see in these examples:

The dog licked it's personal region.
Its not my fault those mango's exploded.

A good way to remember the apostrophe rule is to memorize this simple poem:

To get it right with ease
Simply count the apostrophes
If more than one is there
Something something beware

Q. Is there any way to tell the difference between "they're," "their" and "there"?

A. Not at this time.

Q. What is the correct usage of the word "literally"?

A. Grammatically, it is an infractual correlative and as such it must always be preceded by the parabolical phrase "would of."

Wrong: *I literally would of shit a brick.*
Right: *I would of literally shit a brick.*
Also right: *I would of shit a literal brick.*

Q. When should I use quotation marks?

A. They are used in four situations:
   1. When referring to fried foods:
      Try our "delicious" squirrel fritters.
   2. When identifying organized criminals:
      Police arrested Joseph "Joey Two Sternums" Patchouli in connection with the rash of submarine thefts.
   3. In sanitary exhortations:
      All employees "must" wash they're

hands before returning to "work."

4. When something suspicious is going on:
"Get into my windowless van little girl you'll be safe I won't hurt you," said "Uncle Bob."

THREE "TIPS" FOR EFFECTIVE WRITING

1. Avoid stiff, unnatural, outdated language. Don't be afraid to sound like yourself, or even use humor where appropriate.

   Wrong: *As a motivated individual, it is my sincere desire to obtain the position of employee within you're company.*
   Right: *As a motivated individual, it is my sincere desire to obtain the position of employee within you're company LOL.*

2. When writing fiction, make sure your first sentence "grabs" your readers and makes them want to read more.

   Wrong: *"Hurry!" said Jack.*

133

Right: *"Hurry!" said Harry Potter to the* Hunger Games *woman.*

3. Be concise and to the point, especially when writing to busy people such as are found in Internet comment areas.

   Wrong: *I respectfully disagree with you, and here are some facts supporting my position.*
   Right: *Your a fascist.*

■ ■ ■ ■

AIR TRAVELERS'
FAQ

■ ■ ■ ■

So you're planning to take an airplane trip. Good for you! Every year, millions of people "take to the skies" for business or pleasure, and statistically only a small percentage of them are killed.

Nevertheless, if this is your first flight, or you haven't flown in a while, or you're simply one of the many stupid people found in airports, you're probably unsure about what to expect. So let's review the basics:

Q. I have an infant or small child. Are there any special preparations I should make for flying?

A. Definitely. Before you leave home, gather together whatever toys, books or games you will need to keep your child occupied. Then remain home, occupying your child, until he or she is a minimum of sixteen years old.

Q. When should I leave for the air-port?

A. You should already be at the airport.

Q. Should I check my luggage?

A. That depends on several factors, the main one being: Do you ever want to see your luggage again? Also, how much spare money do you have? Most major airlines are bankrupt, so they now charge hefty fees for checking your bags and other "extras" such as food, oxygen and keeping all the engines turned on for the entire flight. The notable exception is Southwest, which has remained profitable by avoiding costly "frills" such as using professional pilots.

Q. So who is flying the Southwest planes?

A. English majors wearing pilot hats.

Q. What are the "do's" and "don'ts" of airport security screening?

A. We'll start with a "do": Relax! Airport

138

security is handled by the Transportation Security Administration, which is an agency of the federal government (Motto: "A Gigantic Bureaucracy Working for You"). Some TSA procedures may seem ridiculous, but remember this: There are real terrorists out there and it's the TSA's job to make sure that these terrorists do not get on an airplane until they have fully complied with TSA procedures.

FACT: No terrorist has ever boarded a domestic flight with more than 3.4 ounces of toothpaste, as far as we know.

Make sure your carry-on luggage does not contain any prohibited items, including liquids, gels, gases or solids. If you plan to wear underwear, wear it on the *outside* of your other garments so that it is clearly visible to the TSA agents. Remove all shoes, belts, sweaters, coats, hats, wigs, eyeglasses, contact lenses, hearing aids, insulin pumps, artificial limbs, pacemakers and donated organs, such as kidneys, and place these in the bins provided, then shuffle or crawl slowly forward in the security line with your head down, taking care not to appear suspicious or make eye contact with anybody.

The heart of the screening procedure is

when you go into the "scanner," which sounds scary, although, in fact, it's nothing more than a giant microwave oven that bombards your body with atomic radiation. But there's no need to worry: The scanner is completely safe for humans as long as (a) you do not remain in there longer than the recommended eight-tenths of a second and (b) TSA agents have remembered to change the power setting from POPCORN back to HUMANS after their break.

The scanner serves a vital security function: It "sees" through your clothing and captures an image of your naked body, which is transmitted to a room where specially trained TSA agents decide whether to post it on Facebook. If you would prefer not to have this happen, simply ask to have an agent grope your genitals manually. It's your right!

The main "don't" of airport security is: *Don't make inappropriate jokes.* TSA agents are responsible for your safety, so they must take every possible threat seriously; if you engage in inappropriate humor, they have no choice but to shoot you.

Q. How do I know what humor is inappropriate?

A. You should refer to the official TSA guidelines:

*TRANSPORTATION SECURITY ADMINIS-
TRATION CHECKPOINT HUMOR GUIDE-
LINES*

INAPPROPRIATE	APPROPRIATE
"I have a bomb in my backpack."	"I have a bomb in my backpack. Ha-ha! I am just joking around with you in an appropriate manner."
"Knock, knock."	"Knock, knock."
"Who's there?"	"Who's there?"
"Anita."	"Anita."
"Anita who?"	"Anita who?"
"Anita catch a plane, you morons."	"Here is my government-issued photo ID."

Q. How many TSA agents does it take to screw in a lightbulb?

A. Five. One to screw in the bulb, and four to strip-search an elderly paraplegic woman for no apparent reason

Q. How many TSA agents does it take to screw in a lightbulb?

A. That so-called "elderly paraplegic woman" could be concealing an illegal quantity of toothpaste.

Q. What do I do if I make it through security?

A. You should check an airport monitor to determine the status of your flight. If it says "DELAYED," your flight is delayed.

Q. What if it doesn't say "DE-LAYED?"

A. Then your flight has been canceled.

Q. What is the procedure for boarding an airplane?

A. Most airlines board planes by income level, starting with wealthy people and working down the income ladder to the homeless. Make careful note of your boarding group, which will be printed on your boarding pass. Shortly before boarding time, a gate agent will make an announcement telling passengers that to facilitate the boarding process they should not approach the jet bridge until their group has been called. This is the signal for everybody within two hundred yards, including people who are not even on that particular flight, to charge toward the jet bridge as though the plane is the last chopper out of a city overrun by zombies. *You must join this charge* or you will not get an overhead luggage space and they will have to check your suitcase and you will never see it again.

Q. How do I know which seat on the airplane is mine?

A. It will be the one directly in front of the screaming infant.

Q. When the flight attendant announces for the third time that all cell phones must be turned off immediately or the plane cannot leave the gate, does that mean I should

turn my cell phone off?

A. That announcement does not apply to you.

Q. I'm a little nervous about flying. Is this normal?

A. Absolutely! Believe it or not, even many airline crew members admit that flying gives them the "jitters."

Q. How do they handle this?

A. They smoke crack.

Q. What if something goes wrong with the airplane while it's flying?

A. There's nothing to worry about! The pilot will simply land the plane on the Hudson River, where it will float until rescue boats arrive.

Q. What if we're not flying over the Hudson River?

A. Then you will die. Basically, you should restrict your air travel to flights between New York and Albany.

144

Q. But I don't want to go to Albany.

A. Good, because that flight has been canceled.

Q. How do airplanes actually fly, anyway?

A. It may seem like magic, but it's really just basic physics. A fully loaded 747 weighs around 800,000 pounds, which sounds like a lot until you realize that it's actually the same as just 1,231 grand pianos. Scientists tell us that to get this weight off the ground, two forces are required: engine "thrust," which moves the airplane forward until it is going 150 miles per hour, at which point it develops "lift" and rises into the air.

Q. So you're telling me that if I got a grand piano going 150 miles per hour, it would rise into the air?

A. *I'm* not telling you that. *Scientists* are telling you that.

Q. Do you believe them?

A. I believe they travel by train.

■ ■ ■ ■

SEEKING WIFI IN THE HOLY LAND

■ ■ ■ ■

I am not a religious man, but there is one passage in the Old Testament that has always spoken to me. It's in the Book of Ruminations, Chapter 4, Verse 2, Row 2, Seat 6, which states: "In thy sixty-fifth year, thou shalt go into the Land of Israel, and thou shalt travel around to every place in a tour bus filled with Jews."

And so it was that one day in June I set out with my wife, Michelle, and our daughter Sophie from JFK airport, flying to Tel Aviv on El Al.* We were going to join a tour of Israel sponsored by our synagogue, Temple Judea of Coral Gables, FL. This is a Reform congregation that is open-minded enough to allow even me to be a member. I'm not Jewish. Michelle and Sophie are, but I'm not religious at all. The most spiritual thing I do is sometimes, in times of

* Hebrew, meaning, literally, "The Al."

crisis, quietly ask for a Higher Power, if one exists, to intervene in certain crucial field goals. Other than that, the Higher Power and I pretty much leave each other alone.

Michelle and I were both a little nervous about going to Israel, which we viewed as a potentially dangerous place. This is pretty funny when you consider that we live in Miami, which is (a) a place where motorists routinely use firearms as turn signals and (b) the only major U.S. city that has in recent years experienced both a massive Burmese python infestation *and* a cannibal attack.

But Israel seemed scarier to us because it's located smack-dab in the middle of the Middle East, which is not one of the world's mellower regions. Here are some newspaper headlines you will never see:

HO-HUM! ANOTHER QUIET DAY IN MIDDLE EAST

Everybody in Middle East Getting Along Great

And the headline that you will *especially* never see is:

ISRAEL VERY POPULAR WITH NEIGHBORS

150

So we were wondering whether the Israel trip was a wise move, especially when we got to the El Al check-in area at JFK and saw a uniformed man carrying a large military-style rifle, wandering among the passengers as if prepared to obliterate anybody violating the three-ounce limit on carry-on shampoo. Before we checked in, a serious security man asked us a bunch of serious questions about our trip, which we — desperate to convince him that we were not terrorists — responded to like the von Trapp family on cocaine, speaking in unnaturally perky voices while smiling enthusiastically for no discernible reason.

Eventually the security man concluded that we were harmless tourist idiots and let us check in. After passing through several more levels of security we reached the concourse, where I stopped at a change booth to exchange some dollars for Israeli currency. To my surprise, this turned out to be called shekels. I had always thought "shekel" was a jokey slang term for "money," like "moolah." I wondered if I was being made the butt of a prank played on clueless travelers by bored airport change-booth personnel. ("The moron actually accepted 'shekels'! Next time let's see if he'll take 'simoleons.' ")

I pocketed my "shekels" and we proceeded to our gate, where, after one more security check, we boarded an El Al 747 along with what appeared to be the entire population of the East Coast. The flight to Tel Aviv took eleven hours and was uneventful, unless you count the actions of the Airplane Lavatory Blockade Unit (ALBU). This is a highly trained group of operatives who travel on every overseas flight I have ever been on. They wait until everybody else is asleep, then they go into all of the lavatories and close the doors, and they do not come out for the remainder of the flight. I don't know what they do in there. Possibly their income taxes. All I know is, the ALBU does a crackerjack job of preventing me from using the lavatories, which is why I always arrive at my international destination feeling as though I am carrying a mature water buffalo in my intestinal tract.

But the important thing was, we made it to Israel safe and sound, eager for adventure. I would have been less eager if I had known that one of the adventures would involve walking backward off a cliff. But I'm getting ahead of the time line. Let's start at the beginning of my Israel trip diary:

We take a taxi from Ben-Gurion Airport to our hotel. Tel Aviv turns out to be a lot like Miami: It has condos, palm trees, beaches, and drivers who do not believe the traffic laws apply to them personally. Also, nobody is speaking English. But here, instead of Spanish, people speak Hebrew, a language featuring many words that are pronounced as though they are only nanoseconds away from turning into a loogie.

We're staying in a large, modern hotel right next to the Mediterranean. It takes me several minutes to check us in and during this time the water buffalo is making it increasingly clear that it yearns to roam free, if you catch my drift. I really, *really* need to get up to the room. But when I look around, I cannot find Michelle.

Finally, I track her down in the hotel gift shop. I don't mean to reinforce an unfortunate gender stereotype here but my wife is the Navy SEAL Team 6 of shopping. She can strike anywhere, anytime, at a moment's notice. Strap a parachute on this woman and drop her into the remotest part of the Amazon Basin, a place populated only by headhunters still living in the Stone Age, and she will, days later, emerge from the rain forest, staggering, emaciated, bleeding and covered with leeches, but clutching a primitive shopping bag containing a set of souvenir shrunken heads. She will then insist that (1) she got the heads at a good price and (2) they will go really well with our living room.

What Michelle has found in the Tel Aviv hotel gift shop are menorahs, which are ceremonial candleholders used in celebrating the Jewish holiday of Chanukah. At this point, I become cranky because (1) Chanukah is six months away and (2) thanks to Michelle's relentless efforts over the years, we already have (this is a conservative estimate) seventy-five menorahs at home. We could open up our own store, called Menorah World. It does not seem to me, there in the hotel lobby, jet-lagged to a near stupor and with the water buffalo rampaging around in my bowels, that purchasing still *more* menorahs, in the hotel lobby, at this *particular* moment, is an urgent need. Reluctantly, Michelle agrees to leave the shop, which is fortunate because we reach our room just in time to avert a seriously disgusting explosive medical development that would have rendered the entire Middle East uninhabitable for decades.

A short while later, feeling less cranky and, in one case, considerably lighter, we leave

154

the hotel. We have the afternoon off — our organized tour starts tomorrow — so we head for the beach, where we sit down for lunch at an outdoor café. As we gaze upon the beautiful blue waters of the Mediterranean Sea, which has played such a significant role in world history, Sophie makes an observation that reminds us why it is so important to take children along on trips to foreign lands.

"They have free wifi here," she says.

Instantly we grab our phones to check texts, e-mails, tweets, Instagram, Facebook, etc. I know we should be ashamed, but this is what every tourist does. The Messiah could ride a unicycle through a crowded tourist area wearing nothing but a set of bagpipes and if there was free wifi, nobody would notice.

After lunch we walk along a scenic seaside promenade to Jaffa, an ancient port city containing many fascinating historic sights that we ignore because there is also shopping. I personally am in the market for some cheap rubber sandals because we've been told that at some point our tour will involve wading in an ancient underground water tunnel. I find a sidewalk stall where an elderly man is displaying many kinds of footwear, including sandals. I pick up a sandal and show it to the man.

"Forty shekels," he says, in a heavy accent.

At this point, I'm supposed to bargain. All the guide books say so. I'm supposed to offer the man, say, fifteen shekels, and then, in the ancient Middle Eastern tradition, we'll haggle for a while, and finally we will agree on a price. Or we will kill each other's entire families. But the rule of buying in a Middle Eastern market is *never pay the asking price.*

However, I come from a long line of WASPs. Our tradition is to pay full price, then get revenge by starting an exclusive country club. I hate bargaining, and I am terrible at it. Also, forty shekels is around eleven dollars, which to me seems very reasonable for the sandals. So I say OK to the man and hand him a hundred-shekel bill. It is only after we have walked back to our hotel that I realize two things:

(1) The sandals are defective.

(2) He actually charged me eighty shekels for them. Apparently, when I held up the sandal, he quoted me a price for just that one sandal, as if he believed I planned to hop around the Middle East on just the one foot.

I consider marching back to Jaffa and

confronting the sandal man or — this would be truer to my heritage — building a golf course and refusing to let him play there. But it's getting late and we have to meet for dinner with the rest of our tour group, which totals twenty-five people. We eat at a restaurant featuring cuisine from Yemen (National motto: "Even We Don't Know Where It Is"). The dinner is delicious. If for some reason that I cannot personally imagine you ever find yourself in Yemen, my recommendation is: Try the food.

DAY TWO

We start at the hotel with an "Israeli-style" breakfast buffet, which is a vast array of fresh salads, fruits, vegetables, fish, breads, cereals, cheeses and on and on and *on*. Israelis take food very seriously. This is another area where Jews and WASPs differ. Your typical Protestant breakfast buffet consists of a dense mass of scrambled eggs that could have been scrambled during the Clinton administration; for side dishes there will be bacon, potatoes and — for variety — some other kind of potatoes.

After breakfast we lumber outside and board our tour bus. Finally, after months of planning and anticipation, we are setting out on our tour of Israel. There is a feeling of excitement, almost giddiness, among the members of our group, because it turns out that *the bus has wifi.*

Our first stop is Independence Hall, the building in central Tel Aviv, where, on May 14, 1948, with the ruling British about to pull out of what was then called Palestine — an unstable mixture of Arabs and Jews — Israel declared itself to be an independent state. Almost immediately the new nation was attacked by Iraq, Lebanon, Syria, Jordan and Egypt. Basically, the Israelis were fighting all their Arab neighbors at once; it's amazing that that hostile Arab jellyfish didn't crawl out of the Mediterranean and start stinging them.

Israel won that war and survived, but there were more wars in 1956, 1967 and 1973, as well as many other periods of violent conflict, continuing right up until today. Generally the way these conflicts go is . . .

WARNING! WARNING! WARNING!

GROSS OVERSIMPLIFICATION OF COMPLEX ISSUE AHEAD

. . . Israel, which has a kickass army, wins the conflict and in the process captures a bunch of new territory. Then, after interna-

158

tional pressure and lengthy negotiations, there is some kind of historic peace agreement, which usually involves Israel giving at least some of the captured territory back. This agreement is traditionally signed in the presence of whoever happens to be the president of the United States, whose traditional role is to beam ecstatically over the proceedings as though he is at that moment being serviced by an intern. This is followed by a lasting peace that lasts anywhere from fifteen to twenty minutes. Then there is conflict again.

A major source of the conflict is the issue of what to do about the Palestinian Arabs, who want — not without reason — to have their own nation on territory that Israel currently controls. Polls show that most Israelis would be willing to give up land if it meant there would be permanent peace; the concern is that there would not be peace and that a diminished Israel — which even in its current incarnation is about the width of a regulation volleyball court — would be less able to defend itself from its enemies, some of whom have made it clear that the only kind of peace they want with Israel is the kind the Death Star wanted with the Planet Alderaan.

So security is a very, very big issue for

Israelis, even bigger than food. They know that any day could be the day another war starts. Most young Israelis, men and women, serve in the army. (The exception is the ultra-Orthodox, who generally do not serve in the army, a fact that causes a lot of resentment.) Everywhere you go, you see teenagers in uniform carrying assault rifles, which they never set down, even when they're eating. I had mixed reactions to this. On the one hand, I'd think: *We're safe because there are all these soldiers around.* On the other hand, I'd think: *Wait a minute: Why are all these soldiers around?*

But getting back to our tour of Independence Hall: The highlight is an emotional talk about the birth and desperate early struggles of Israel, given by a tough Israeli woman guide — she *shushes* a boisterous group of American college students and they shut right up — in the room where Israel's independence was declared. At the end of her talk, she plays a recording of Israel's founding father and first prime minister, David Ben-Gurion, proclaiming the establishment of the Jewish independent state, his voice being broadcast to the new nation via the microphone that still sits today on the long table at the front of the room. Then we stand, and those who know the words sing the Israeli national anthem, "Hatikvah" ("The Hope"). At this point, Michelle is (1) bawling and (2) ready to join the Israeli army. She would serve in the elite Shopping Corps.

After leaving Independence Hall, we travel to a town just outside Tel Aviv, where we tour a secret munitions factory that was operated from 1946 to 1948 by Haganah, the Zionist paramilitary organization that was fighting for an independent Jewish state when the British controlled Palestine. Haganah could get guns but had trouble obtaining ammunition, so it built an underground factory, hidden beneath the laundry of a kibbutz that was essentially just a front to fool the British. There, forty-five young people, working under harsh and dangerous conditions, manufactured more than two million bullets. Had they been caught, they would have faced the death penalty. It's a fascinating tour. Some of us don't even check to see if there's wifi.

We get back on the bus and head south, into the Negev Desert. Along the way we get some more history from our tour guide, Doron Wilfand, who was born and raised on a kibbutz and served in the army. He graduated from Hebrew University and did postgraduate work in religious studies at

Duke, where he developed a taste for American sports, especially pro football, which he knows more about than we do.

Doron is a sweet, patient, compassionate and very smart guy. He is also unbelievably well informed. He does not do tour guide patter. Whatever you ask him about, he gives you a thoughtful, nuanced, nondogmatic and encyclopedically detailed answer, sometimes including personal anecdotes. If you ask him, for example, about the Israeli–Palestinian conflict, he'll give you an articulate twenty-minute argument for the Palestinian position, at the end of which you will feel (if you are me) suddenly pro-Palestinian. But then he will give an equally articulate twenty-minute argument for the Israeli position, and you will feel (if you are me) suddenly very much of two minds. Then he will present a *third* way of looking at the conflict, and then a fourth, and maybe a fifth, until your brain is throbbing from looking at the issue from so many different perspectives and you realize that the only thing you will ever really understand about the Middle East is that you will never really understand the Middle East.

On the other hand, as far as I can tell, nobody in the Middle East really does, either.

As we drive south, Israel quickly becomes a desert — miles and miles of sunbaked dirt and rocks. There are also occasional roadside camels, which stand around acting as though it is perfectly normal for them to be by the side of the road, as opposed to in a circus.

Finally, we reach our destination, which is a Bedouin camp. The Bedouin are tribal, traditionally desert-dwelling Arabs; there are more than one hundred thousand of them in Israel. They pretty much keep to themselves, but they are Israeli citizens; some of them even join in the Israel Defense Forces, where they serve as trackers.

This particular camp is essentially a tourist attraction. You can ride camels there, have a Bedouin-style meal and even spend the night in a tent. There are several busloads of American college students staying in the tents. They're with Birthright Israel, a nonprofit program that brings Jewish young adults to Israel for free ten-day trips, during which they learn about their cultural and religious heritage. Because they are college students, some of them also take the opportunity (although this is not a formal part of the program) to get hammered.

We are not, thank God, spending the night in tents with the college students. We're

163

there to ride camels. I am not thrilled about this. I do not enjoy climbing onto the backs of large animals (horses are another example) that have hard feet and could, anytime they wanted, throw me off and stomp me until my skeletal system was the consistency of rice pudding. If I were a camel and hefty American tourists kept climbing onto *my* back, I would definitely try to kill them. No jury could convict me. I would plead camel.

The Bedouin are operating a camel train, consisting of fifteen camels tied together in a line. Each camel carries two people on a big saddle. The train makes about a fifteen-minute loop, going out into the desert and back. There is no beverage cart service.

Before we board, we receive a short briefing from a Bedouin named Amir, who gives us these instructions:

- "Don't get with food on you on the camel. The camel behind you will try to eat it."

- "Hold on tight. The camels are coming up and down a little bit funny."

- "Don't pet the camel. They don't like to be pet."

- "Try to avoid screaming."

Two Bedouin guys herd the camel train over to our group and make the camels kneel. Michelle and I board the last camel in the train. A Bedouin does something to make the camel stand and, *WHOA*, Amir was not kidding about coming up funny. It is all I can do to observe the no-screaming rule as we lurch violently upward to a height of (this is an estimate) seventy-five feet.

Then the camel train starts moving and, *WHOA*, we discover why you never hear camels described as "The Lexus Luxury Sedans of the Desert." It is not a smooth ride. It's like a rockin' and rollin' amusement park attraction called the Krazy Kamel. We're going maybe two miles an hour, but Michelle and I are clinging to the saddle like terrified barnacles.

To make matters worse, our camel, which we nickname "Thunderbolt," has decided that he* no longer wishes to be the last camel in the train. He keeps trying to pass the camel in front of us. Maybe he's tired of being the fifteenth camel, spending all day schlepping tourists around a loop and staring at the butt of the fourteenth camel. He has ambitions! He wants to move up in life,

* I'm assuming Thunderbolt is a he.

165

maybe stare at the butt of the thirteenth camel or even (He can dream, can't he?) the butt of the twelfth camel.

Whatever the reason, Thunderbolt keeps speeding up to 2.1 miles per hour and attempting to pass. The ropes prevent him from succeeding, but he is not the kind of camel to give up easily, so, as we jounce along, we repeatedly bang into Camel 14. The Bedouin guys don't seem to notice. Michelle keeps asking me — because naturally, as the husband, I am supposed to be an authority on camel behavior — "Is it supposed to do this?" We are involved in numerous camel collisions as we jolt our way around the loop. We are greatly relieved when we finish and, *WHOA,* Thunderbolt kneels to let us off. My feeling is if this is how people have been getting around for centuries, no wonder the Middle East is tense.

After the camel ride we go into a big tent, sit on mats on the floor and enjoy a hearty meal featuring a specialty of Bedouin cuisine: Roast Hump.

No, seriously, we did not eat camel. As far as I know. It was dark in the tent.

After dinner we drive to a very nice hotel in a town called Mitzpe, right next to the famous Ramon Crater, which — as you know if, like me, you just looked it up on Wikipedia — is "a large erosion cirque." Our hotel is perched on a rock ledge overlooking a vast desert valley. From our room, as the sun sets, we can see a dramatic rock cliff plunging straight down a long, *lonnnng* way to the valley floor. Looking at it, I recall that the tour schedule for tomorrow involves rappelling. But I am sure that there is no way that anybody would expect a bunch of tourist schlubs like us — people from Miami-Dade County, where the highest point, by far, is a landfill — to rappel down this *particular* cliff. Surely we'll be using some smaller, wussier cliff, right? *Right?* This is what is on my mind as the sun goes down.

Fortunately, the hotel has a bar.

DAY THREE

After another traditional 273-course Israeli breakfast, our group climbs into four Land Rovers for a trip into the crater. From the hotel the highway descends through a series of switchbacks about a thousand feet to the crater floor. In a few miles we turn off the road onto a barely there dirt track and start lurching up a steep, rocky hill. There is no vegetation anywhere, just rocks and dirt. The driver tells us we are in what is called extreme desert. He says it gets very hot here, but he gives the temperature in Celsius, so all we hear is a meaningless number such as "fourteen" or "thirty-eight." We ask him how hot it gets in *real* degrees and he launches into a brief rant in favor of the metric system, ending with, "You Americans, with the inches and the yards! Grow up!"

After driving upward through a great deal of nothing, we arrive at a high vantage point from which we can see: a whole lot more nothing. We get out of our Land Rovers, and the main crater guide explains where we are.

"You are in the middle of nowhere," he says. "If you want to live here, you are in trouble."

We have no desire to live there, but we do take numerous pictures of ourselves standing in front of the nothing in various groupings. Then we pile back into the Land Rovers for a rocky, bouncy drive down a series of tracks and through miles and miles of desert until finally we reach our destination, which is: a tree. I am pretty sure this is the only tree in the Negev Desert. If you look closely at a map of southern Israel and you see a tiny dot labeled "Tree," that is our location.

We pile out of the Land Rovers again and gather around the guide, who squats by the tree and uses a pile of sand, some bottled water and a stick to demonstrate the geological process that formed the Ramon Crater. As I understand it, what happened was, there was this huge raised area of land that was eroded over millions of years by water being poured from a giant plastic bottle. It occurs to me that the reason why the Negev Desert Tree is located here is that this particular spot has been watered by thousands of tour guide demonstrations.

Before we leave the Negev Desert Tree, we spend a few minutes tossing a football — one of the families brought it along — with the drivers. They're not sure how to throw it, but they have seen enough NFL on TV to perfectly mimic a quarterback hunching over a center and barking out nonsensical sounds. One of the drivers says: "What's up with the Dolphins? No Dan Marino?"

Even in the middle of nowhere, we can't escape the pain.

After the crater tour there is an optional tour of an alpaca farm. I don't really know what "alpacas" are and I don't want to run the risk that they're anything like camels, so I pass on the tour. This is a decision I will come to regret because if I *had* gone to the alpaca farm and an alpaca *had* decided to stomp me to death, I would have gotten out of participating in the next scheduled tour activity, which is: rappelling.

We walk from the hotel to the rappelling site, which turns out to be the very same cliff that I observed the night before from the hotel room: the Cliff of Death. I seriously would like to get out of this — I'm afraid of heights — but I can't think of a manly way to back down in front of my daughter, who thinks this is a *great* idea. I reassure myself with the thought that the rappelling company surely must have a facility with a trained professional staff and many safety procedures.

What they have is: a guy.

One guy. He's standing casually right on the edge of the cliff, his back to the crater, his heels practically hanging over the ledge. Because of the angle, it looks to me as though he's thousands of feet above the floor of the valley behind him. I'm scared just *looking* at him, but he does not appear to be even a tiny bit concerned.

There is no rappelling facility. There is a metal ring bolted into the rock near the cliff edge and some harnesses scattered on the ground. The guy tells us to put the harnesses on, then gives us a briefing on how to rappel.

In the United States, where we have a ratio of 4.7 lawyers for every human, the briefing would have lasted at least an hour and we would have signed legal indemnity forms until our fingers bled, admitting that we were suicidal idiots for engaging in this insanely dangerous activity and legally indemnifying the rappelling company from every bad thing that could ever possibly happen to us, including lightning strikes, earthquakes, comets, werewolf attacks and of course loss of blood caused by signing the forms.

But here, on the Cliff of Death, there is no paperwork to sign. The briefing takes maybe three minutes. Basically, the guy tells us that we will be walking backward off the cliff. He says we have nothing to worry about because we'll be attached to ropes.

"It's safer than riding in a car," he says. This is not a reassuring statement for people who live in Miami. For us, smearing our bodies with pig blood and playing water polo in a shark tank is also safer than riding in a car, but that's not an argument for actually *doing* it.

After giving us the brief briefing, the rappelling guy asks who wants to go first. Our fearless group leader, Rabbi Edwin "Eddie" Goldberg, immediately volunteers. He walks backward off the cliff and, with a jaunty wave, falls to his death.

No, that's what I expect to happen, but somehow Rabbi Eddie makes it to the bottom alive. He remains at the base of the cliff to untie the people who follow. A teenage boy goes next; I can see his legs and arms shaking with terror as he backs off the cliff. But he also makes it down OK. The rappelling guy asks for the next volunteer and I step forward — not because I am suddenly brave but because I know that if I wait any longer, I will back out of this and Sophie will think I'm a coward. Which, make no mistake, is what I am. I just don't want Sophie *thinking* it.

So I walk up to the cliff edge. You know how — I'm talking to you men now — when you meet a well-endowed woman wearing a low-cut garment, you make a major effort to maintain eye contact with her because you don't want her to think you're thinking about her breasts, which are of course all you're thinking about? That's how I handle the cliff. The cliff is a giant set of bazooms and I am determined not to look at it. I am making *intense* eye contact with the rappelling guy. He probably thinks that at any moment I'm going to ask him out. He attaches the ropes to me and gives me some final instructions — I have no idea what he's saying — then tells me to start walking backward off the cliff. Which I do, still maintaining eye contact with him.

"You have to look where you're putting your feet," he says. Reluctantly, I look down and . . .

WHOA.

This is way, *way* worse than the camel. My brain, which has spent all these years trying to keep me alive, cannot *believe* what my idiot feet have gotten me into. It is shrieking at me to go back up. Meanwhile, the rappelling guy keeps telling me to lean back. I don't want to lean back; I want to grab the cliff and hug it tightly. I want to become so intimate with the cliff that a few months from now it has little cliff babies that look like me.

The rappelling guy keeps giving me instructions. I am slowly making my way down the cliff, but I am still terrified to the point of sphincter malfunction. From directly below, I hear Rabbi Eddie shouting words of encouragement. An alarming thought flashes across my brain. I don't know what the laws of Israel are, but I can picture this headline:

This is me and the rappelling guy at the top of the cliff. Note that I am not looking at the cliff. "Cliff?" I am telling myself. "*What* cliff?" My shorts are unsoiled at this time.

(Photo by Doug Shapiro)

AMERICAN TOURIST
FACES DEATH PENALTY

Pooped on Rabbi While Rappelling

Somehow I make it to the bottom without dying or soiling myself or anybody else. I am trembling, but feeling proud. This feeling lasts for about ninety seconds, which is how long it takes for Sophie to scoot down the cliff — smiling hugely the whole way — then ask if we can do it again. I assure her that we will absolutely do it again just as soon as our legs are rested and there are Walmarts on Jupiter.

After rappelling we walk, some of us shakily, back to the hotel for drinks and dinner, and several more drinks. After dinner Doron has an idea, which is that we should (why not?) experience the desert at night. So we all pile onto the bus and head back down into the crater. We drive for about fifteen minutes, then pull off the road. We pile out of the bus and begin experiencing the desert at night.

Here's the main thing about the desert at night: It's dark. We can't see anything. Doron, who apparently has sonar, leads us, tripping and stumbling, up a rocky invisible path away from the road to an even darker part of the desert. He tells us he wants us to separate, to go off into the desert on our own for a while to look at the stars and meditate in solitude. We separate until we are, as a group, approximately two inches apart because nobody really wants to be separated out here at night with God knows what kind of lurking predatory nocturnal desert creatures such as vampire alpacas.

In our Clump of Solitude, we gaze at the stars for a while — there are a LOT of stars — and then Doron has us form a circle so we can express what we are feeling. We go around the circle and express a variety of deep thoughts, mostly along the lines of: Wow, the universe! Then Doron uses his sonar to lead us out of there. He reminds me of Moses, leading the Israelites out of Egypt until finally, after much hardship and many years of wandering around the desert, they reached the tour bus. And God gave them wifi.

DAY FOUR

After a hearty traditional Israeli breakfast, we have our stomachs pumped and board the bus, which takes us to Masada. This ancient, awesome fortress, on a high rock plateau overlooking the Dead Sea, is a major tourist attraction and an important symbol for Israelis: It was here, according to legend, that in 73 A.D. a group of 960 Jewish rebels — men, women and children — who had been holding out against a siege by Roman troops, chose to commit suicide rather than be captured alive. In our group, we get to speculating on how the rebels could possibly have brought themselves to kill their own families. One of the dads, Tony Menninger, says: "Having been penned up with my family on a long car ride . . ."

We hike to the top of Masada, where Doron fills us in on the history and we take several thousand redundant photographs of the view. We then proceed to a small pavilion near the edge of the plateau. There, with the help of a rented Torah (you can rent Torahs on Masada), Rabbi Eddie conducts a bar/bat mitzvah service for two of the young people on our tour, Leo Menninger and Jamie Shapiro. It's far less formal than these services usually are — we're in shorts and T-shirts — but it's moving, and the setting is spectacular, here in this historic place, with the Dead Sea far below in the distance.

The only glitch comes when the parents read a prayer titled "To Be Recited by Parents Celebrating a Child's Becoming Bar/Bat Mitzvah in Israel." The parents fail to notice that the prayer book, although it's written in English, is set up Hebrew style, meaning the pages are numbered in the opposite direction. So when the parents reach the bottom of page 57, instead of going to the top of page 58, they go to the top of page *56,* which puts them in the middle of a different prayer, this one meant to be recited "For Israeli Soldiers or Civilians Being Held Captive." All of a sudden the parents are asking God to "Send complete rescue and full redemption to those held captive by the enemy." This seems kind of grim for a bar mitzvah. Fortunately, Rabbi Eddie catches the mistake and gets the parents back on course; the service ends happily, with hugs and many more pictures.

We take a cable car down to the base of Masada, where, to Michelle's delight, there is a gift shop that Doron describes, accurately, as "the size of the rest of Israel." There are also a number of restaurants, including a McDonald's. After eating and purchasing various hugely unnecessary things, we get back on the bus and motor a short distance to the Dead Sea.

The Dead Sea is a super-salty inland sea whose shore is the lowest dry-land place on Earth. Tourists have been bathing in it for centuries and for a very good reason: Tourists are idiots. No, really. For some reason, when we leave home and join tour groups, we instantly degenerate to the same level of brain function as watermelons. We can be talked into doing *anything.* Walking backward off cliffs, for example.

In the case of the Dead Sea, what we have is a vast pool of warm, oily liquid (allegedly water, though I have my doubts). We ought to be able to figure out from the name "Dead Sea" alone that we should stay the hell out of it. Fish have figured this out; even *plants* have figured this out. But not us tourists! We walk cheerfully past a sign that says:

Do NOT jump or dive into the water

Do NOT immerse your head

Do NOT splash water on yourself or others

Do NOT drink seawater — if you swallow seawater, request help from the life guard or first aid provider

In other words, the sign is saying: *Turn back now, you fool.* But we do not turn back. We're tourists! We walk right up to the Dead

179

Sea and we smear Dead Sea mud on our bodies because . . . We don't know why! But all the other tourists are doing it! If they were stuffing Dead Sea sand into their nostrils, we'd do that, too!

After we smear on our mud, we go into the Dead Sea and, as millions of tourists have done before us, we marvel at how easily we float. Our upper bodies are bobbing *way* out of the water. We're excited and amazed. It doesn't occur to us that *this is not normal.* This is exactly why the fish left. The fish were, like, *WHOA, dude, this is WAY too floaty.*

But we idiot human tourists bob happily away and pose for pictures, lying on our backs and pretending to read a newspaper. Ha-ha! Dead Sea fun!

But then as the initial excitement wears off, we begin to notice that every little cut or scrape on our body is stinging. Then we notice that other sensitive areas, our various bodily crevices and orifices, are also starting to sting. In fact, they're stinging a *lot.* Especially our butts. Our butts are shouting at our brains: *Get out of this toxic stew, you moron.* That's right: As tourists, our IQs have declined to the point where *the most intelligent organ in our body is our asshole.*

So we get out, rinse as much of the Dead Sea off as we can in the outdoor showers and, with butts still stinging, rejoin Doron, our highly knowledgeable guide, who, for the record, has not gotten within a hundred yards of the Dead Sea. We get back onto the bus and head for the city where we'll be spending the next four nights: Jerusalem.

Jerusalem is often called the Las Vegas of the Middle East because of its many casinos and strip clubs.

No, I'm kidding. Jerusalem is an extremely holy city. *Everybody* came through here at one time or another: Moses, Jesus, Muhammad, possibly L. Ron Hubbard. You can't wave your arms in Jerusalem without striking a place or thing that is revered by one or more major world religions, so whatever you do, do *not* wave your arms. There are many intensely religious people walking around here; sometimes, there is tension. And by "sometimes" I mean "pretty much nonstop for several thousand years."

There is also, I regret to report, shopping.

We check into our hotel and after dinner we set off on foot for the Old City, which is divided into the Muslim Quarter, the Christian Quarter, the Jewish Quarter and the Armenian Quarter. I never did get a clear explanation on why the Armenians have a quarter. I mean, nothing against the Armenians, but it seems kind of random, doesn't it? I mean, why doesn't Yemen have a quarter? Or, for that matter, Wisconsin?

We go to the Muslim Quarter, where Doron leads us through a tunnel that runs underground along the Western Wall. The Western Wall is important to Jews because it is a remnant of the ancient wall that surrounded the Temple Mount, which is considered the holiest place in Judaism. The first Jewish temple stood here, before it was destroyed by the Babylonians. The second temple also stood here; it was destroyed by the Romans. Jewish tradition holds that a third and final temple should be built here. The problem is that when the Muslims conquered Jerusalem in the seventh century, they built a shrine, the Dome of the Rock — it's the third-holiest place in Islam — right on top of Temple Mount.

Fortunately, all of these events happened centuries ago. Tempers have cooled since then, so the Jews and Muslims will undoubtedly let bygones be bygones and work out a solution for sharing this holy place that satisfies everybody.

Ha-ha! I am kidding again. In this part of the world, no matter how long ago something happened, plenty of people are still hacked off about it. "Bygones, schmygones," that is the official motto of the Middle East.

We get back to the hotel quite late, exhausted from a long day that began in the desert, took us to the majestic heights of Masada and then to the lowest place on Earth, and ended in a sacred part of one of the world's most ancient, historic and spiritually significant cities. Little wonder that as I finally drift off to sleep the last thought that goes through my mind is: *My butt still stings.*

DAY FIVE

This is not an easy morning. We visit Yad Vashem, the official Israeli memorial to the victims of the Holocaust. It's very well done, managing to convey the horrifying scale of the mass murders without ever letting you lose sight of the fact that every victim was an individual person, with a unique life and spirit. The most moving exhibits, for me, are videos in which survivors describe, matter-of-factly, what was done to them and their loved ones solely because they were Jews. After two hours I walk out into the bright sunlight with tears streaming down my face, holding tight to my daughter.

My Jewish daughter.

From this somber place we go to one of the liveliest places in Jerusalem: the Mahane Yehuda open-air market, which is bustling with people buying food for Shabbat, the day of rest that begins at sundown Friday and ends at sundown Saturday. This is a big part of the Jewish week and it of course involves eating. Michelle finds a store called Kippa Man, where she buys — you cannot have too many — souvenir yarmulkes. We eat lunch at a falafel stand that claims to sell the best falafel in Israel.

FACT: *Every* falafel stand in Israel claims to sell the best falafel in Israel.

FACT: And *every one does.*

In the evening our group attends Shabbat services in a suburb of Jerusalem at Kehilat Mevasseret Zion, a reform synagogue led by Rabbi Maya Leibovitch, the first Israeli-born woman rabbi. After the service, our group breaks into smaller groups, which go to have Shabbat dinner at the homes of members of the congregation. We and another family from the tour go to the small, neat home of Kay and Adi Elkayam, a couple in their sixties. Kay was born in Philadelphia and came to Israel as an adult; Adi is a native Israeli. She's a talker and quite funny; he's quiet and just as funny. (When I ask him how he met Kay, he

184

answers, without elaborating: "By mistake.")

They serve us a massive and delicious meal, during which Kay tells us in no uncertain terms what she thinks about Israeli politics, the Middle East in general, religion, U.S. politics and many other topics. During this time Adi is silent, plodding back and forth between the kitchen and the dining table, bringing us more and more and still more food. Finally, he stops next to Kay and announces: "I do not agree with her." (*Pause.*) "About anything."

After dinner we sit on a circle of chairs in their backyard, talking, drinking wine and enjoying the pleasantly cool evening. We can hear music in the distance; Adi tells us it's a wedding celebration in an Arab neighborhood about a thousand yards away. After a while we hear popping sounds — first a few, then many. We ask if these are fireworks. Adi, who served in the Israeli army, says no, it's celebratory wedding gunfire, but we needn't worry because they're shooting blanks. We ask him if he's sure and he says he is. He describes in some detail the type of blanks traditionally used for weddings. So we go back to talking and drinking wine, with the music and the shooting providing background ambience. It's a fine and festive night.

Much of Jerusalem shuts down for Shabbat, so we're mostly on our own today. Rabbi Eddie leads a small group of us back to the Old City, where we visit the Church of the Holy Sepulchre, by tradition the site where Jesus was crucified and buried. It's packed, thronging with tour groups and believers. Near the entrance dozens of people — many praying fervently, some crying — kneel on the floor, touching or pressing religious objects against the Stone of Anointing, a slab of rock said to be where Jesus was prepared for burial. There's a long line of people waiting to enter an enclosure containing what is said to be the tomb where Jesus was buried. I do my best, trying to recall long-ago Sunday-school lessons, to explain the crucifixion/resurrection story to Sophie. I do not sound convincing to myself, which I guess is why I stopped being religious.

We leave the church, working our way out through the steady flow of incoming tour groups, and head toward the Muslim Quarter. We wander through the Arab market, a maze of narrow stone streets where people in hundreds of tiny stalls wish to sell you — always at a special price — a vast array of items, including jewelry, hats, scarves, plates, spices, knickknacks that achieve truly profound levels of uselessness, hookahs and of course T-shirts. Some of the T-shirts reflect the Arab viewpoint on Mideast issues. One has an image of the Google search page, with "Israel" typed into the search box. Underneath that it says:

Did you mean: PALESTINE

The vendors also sell a wide variety of religious souvenirs, including crucifixes, anointing oil, frankincense, Holy Land ashtrays and crowns of thorns. Really. If you are looking to enhance your home décor with a crown of thorns, the Arab market is the place for you.

BONUS: The Arab market has wifi.

We leave the Arab market and spend the afternoon wandering around Jerusalem. Tragically, because of Shabbat, all the higher-end stores are closed. Try to imagine my pain.

DAY SEVEN

Finally, I get to use my defective forty-shekel-apiece rubber sandals as we tour Hezekiah's Tunnel. This is an underground aqueduct that was hacked through solid rock several thousand years ago by ancient workers who I bet would have been highly amused if they'd known that tourists would one day pay actual money to go down in there. It's a claustrophobically narrow, clammy tunnel, a third of a mile long; the water is up to your knees and sometimes higher. There are no guides, no handrails, no place to stop and rest, no lighting. You are given a tiny key chain flashlight, which inadequately pierces the pitch-blackness ahead of you as you slosh your way through the chilly water, keeping a wary eye out for the Giant Hairy Aqueduct-Dwelling Spider and the Fanged Underwater Alpaca of Death, which as far as I know are imaginary creatures, but they are easy enough to imagine down in Hezekiah's Tunnel.

We finally emerge from the tunnel and hike up to the exposed, aboveground section of the Western Wall. This is the famous part of the wall, a site sacred to Jews because of its proximity to the Temple Mount. The plaza in front of the wall is separated by a screen into two sections: one for men only and a smaller one for women only.

The vibe at the wall is a strange combination of vacation joviality and religious fervor. Some people are there strictly as tourists, smiling and laughing as they pose

188

for photos with the wall as a backdrop as if it were the Washington Monument. Other people, a few feet away, are worshipping intently, praying and rocking back and forth for long periods of time, walking backward when they leave so as not to turn their backs on the wall. Most people, tourists and worshippers alike, write prayers or notes on pieces of paper, which they stick into cracks between the stones. Even I leave a note,* although I feel a little silly.

We spend about an hour at the wall and, moved by the experience, decide to spend the afternoon in quiet contemplation, by which I mean: shopping. We go to the Jewish street market, which you will be relieved to learn has wifi. Michelle finds a number of items that she is able to obtain at a special price and that will go really well with our living room.

While Michelle shops, I observe the throngs of tourists thronging around. Most are American. It used to be that you could tell which tourists were Americans by the fact that they always wore brand-new white sneakers. I am pleased to report that this is no longer the case. Now you can tell them because they always wear brand-new white

* None of your business.

sneakers *and* brand-new sun hats. Apparently word got around to the American tourist community — maybe there are big warning signs in the sneaker stores — that they must at all costs protect themselves from the deadly foreign sun because I'm seeing tour groups in which every single person is wearing either a brand-new sun hat with a floppy brim or — for maximum protection and timeless elegance — one of those sportsperson hats with the long bill sticking out the front and a big fashionable flap hanging down in the back. Take *that,* deadly foreign sun!

Our evening activity is a lecture at the hotel on "The Labyrinth of Israeli Politics" by Reuven Hazan, a ninth-generation Israeli who's a professor of political science at Hebrew University and a very sharp, funny guy. He talks, rapid-fire, for an hour, writing with colored markers on a big pad of paper to help us understand the Israeli political situation. It's complicated because (a) Israel is a democracy with a parliamentary system and proportional representation and (b) no two Israelis (remember Kay and Adi?) agree on anything. The result is that, instead of two big parties, they have many smaller parties, which means that sometimes extremists and lunatics can wield considerable power. As opposed to the American system, where . . .

OK, never mind.

DAY EIGHT

We're back on the bus, leaving Jerusalem and heading north in the Jordan Valley. Our first stop, near the Jordanian border south of the Sea of Galilee, is Kibbutz Sde Eliyahu, which was founded in 1938 by German Zionists. We get an orientation lecture from a kibbutz member, who tells us that many Israeli kibbutzes have privatized and gone into nonagricultural businesses such as manufacturing. ("Almost everybody's toilet in the world has a piece that comes from a kibbutz in Israel," she says.) But Kibbutz Sde Eliyahu is still an old-school socialist agricultural kibbutz, where nobody gets a salary; the idea is that people do what they can and are given what they need.

We tour the fields, where the kibbutz grows a variety of crops using a range of innovative organic farming methods that I would describe to you in fascinating detail except we would both fall asleep. The kibbutz also grows date palms, which are pretty interesting for a plant because — unlike other trees and many married couples —

191

they have sex. Really. According to the kibbutz guide, there are male date palms and female date palms, and in order for a female to have little baby dates, she has to be inseminated by a male. Few sights in nature are more dramatic than a date palm forest at the height of rutting season, resounding with thunderous crashes and splinters the size of harpoons whistling through the air as a pair of male palms clash over a female.

OK, to be honest, I don't know how date palms have sex in the wild. The guide tells us that at the kibbutz, the females are inseminated by people standing on ladders. This reminds me of the joke about the mouse in the jungle who pulls a thorn out of an elephant's foot, then demands payment in the form of sex, but since there are young people on the tour bus I keep my mouth shut.*

At the end of the tour, the guide tells us about an agriculture-related sideline that the kibbutz has gotten into: selling specialized insects. She brings out two boxes, one containing bees (this product is called BioBee) and one containing tiny flies (BioFly). Your BioBees are a mellow, laid-back type of bee, so they're less likely than

* The punch line is "Take it all, bitch."

normal bees to sting you when they pollinate your tomatoes. Your BioFlies kill other flies that you don't want eating your crops. They are tiny Terminators. So if you're an organic type of individual who is in the market for a box o' bugs, Sde Eliyahu is the kibbutz for you.

They also, Michelle discovers, have a gift shop.

We leave the kibbutz and head north, stopping for lunch at a sleepy strip mall with a few deserted stores, a falafel stand and a McDonald's. My family, which has become addicted, goes for the falafel. It's the best in Israel.

As we're eating at an outdoor table, an IDF vehicle with four soldiers inside pulls up to the curb next to us. A young soldier — he looks eighteen — gets out, goes to the falafel stand, buys a pack of cigarettes and returns to the vehicle. This takes him maybe a minute and he is never more than twenty feet from the vehicle. But he has his rifle with him the whole time. This doesn't make us nervous; we're getting used to seeing soldiers. But it's a reminder that Israel has to always be ready. Always.

We resume heading north. The countryside gets greener as we drive along the western side of the Sea of Galilee. We pass marinas, resorts and beaches; unlike the Sea of Butt Sting, the Sea of Galilee contains actual water.

We drive up high into the hills and stop at the picturesque and historic town of Tsfat, which is a center of Kabbalah, a mystical branch of Judaism that became fashionable in Hollywood in the 1990s; its best-known celebrity follower is Madonna. Tsfat is one of Israel's holiest cities, and is a place rich in history. Tragically, it is also a place rich in shopping, offering for sale at a special price many items that would go really well with our living room. While Michelle and Sophie investigate this facet of Tsfat, I find a little stone amphitheater, where I sit to rest my weary legs and contemplate the eternal question of whether or not there is free wifi. (No.) As I'm sitting there, an American tour group walks into the amphitheater and sits down. Their Israel guide gives them a little talk on the history of the Jewish mystical tradition, which dates back centuries. When he's done, he leads the group out. The last two to leave are a young man and a young woman, who have this conversation:

Man: You should take a picture of this.
Woman: Why?

Man: You didn't hear what he said?
Woman: What?
Man: Madonna lives here!

We spend the night at a pleasant hotel in the Hula Valley operated by Kibbutz Kfar Blum. After dinner, Rabbi Eddie brings out his guitar; he and I entertain the tour group with a medley of classic oldies from the sixties and seventies, when we were young and had many more brain cells. Our act consists of one of us saying, "I got one!" then grabbing the guitar and playing anywhere from seven to twenty-three percent of a classic oldie before reaching the point where he can no longer remember the words or the chords, or both. Then the other one will go, "I got one!" grab the guitar and play another classic oldie fragment. Soon the floor in front of us is littered with the corpses of unfinished songs. It is a wild and crazy night, a raucous rock 'n' roll riot, Hula Valley style, and it does not end until nearly 10:27 p.m.

DAY NINE

We drive north toward the Golan Heights and the borders with Lebanon and Syria. There has been a lot of fighting over this territory in decades past, so I'm expecting a battled-scarred wasteland. Instead, it's the most beautiful scenery we've seen so far — mountains, hills, streams, rivers, forests, wildflowers. It reminds us of the North Carolina mountains, except for the roadside signs warning you to stay on the road because of minefields. This is a popular vacation area for Israelis and tourists alike. The borders have been mostly peaceful for a while, although, as Doron points out, "In one day, everything could become very problematic again."

We stop at a hillside overlook, which, instead of overlooking a scenic vista, over-looks Syria. At the moment there's a hor-rific civil war going on in Syria; a week earlier, Doron tells us, there was a battle, involving tanks, in the valley right below us. He gives us an explanation of the Syrian situation, which all of us — here, I speak confidently for the group — find utterly incomprehensible.

In the distance, we hear a *BOOM*.

"That's artillery," says Doron.

"Check, please," says Rabbi Eddie, and we get back on the bus.

We drive a few miles, passing Israeli tanks along the way, to our next tour stop, which — perfectly symbolizing the surreal juxtaposition of military outpost and modern consumer society that is Israel — is a gourmet chocolate factory. There, a factory guide shows us an instructional video, *How Chocolate Is Made.* It all begins with the cacao tree, which produces beans after having sex with a male date palm.

No, seriously, the way they make chocolate is, they do various instructional things to cacao beans until they turn into chocolate. After watching the video, we tour the factory, then put on paper hats and, using ingredients provided by our guide, try our hand at making and decorating our own chocolates. Despite the fact that we're amateurs, we manage to produce a variety of creative, personalized confections that look remarkably like cow turds with names dribbled on them. This does not stop us from eating them. Because, dammit, we're *tourists.*

Our final activity for the day is rafting on the Jordan River. This is another one of those activities that in the United States would be preceded by form signing and a safety lecture, and would probably involve a guide. Here, we basically pile into rubber rafts and shove off, on our own. The river is crowded. It's rush hour for rafts on the Jordan Expressway. Some are Jewish rafts and some are Arab rafts, but everybody's in a good mood. We're all using our paddles to splash one another — Jews splashing Jews, Arabs splashing Arabs, Jews splashing Arabs, Arabs splashing Jews. Along the riverbanks, people are hanging out, barbecuing and smoking hookahs. It's a totally mellow scene.

It occurs to me, as we drift along, that maybe the way to achieve lasting peace in the Middle East is to take the leaders of the various hostile nations and put them together in a raft out here on the Jordan River. Call me a dreamer, but I bet that after an hour or so of drifting amid that happy throng of rafters — seeing all these ordinary people of different religions and ethnic backgrounds getting along, having fun together, without animosity or hatred — these leaders would find a way, somehow, to kill one another with their paddles.

So never mind.

DAY TEN

This day begins with one of the most dramatic events in the history of Israel, if not the entire world.

Michelle, who has been following the developments on her phone, wakes me up at 6 a.m. with the shocking news: The Miami Heat, trailing three games to two in the NBA finals, are in danger of losing Game 6, and the championship, to the San Antonio Spurs.

I am not the kind of man to panic in an emergency. Calmly, I leap out of bed, turn on the TV, find the game — which is being broadcast in Hebrew — and begin shouting at the screen. Despite my efforts, the game does not go well. With less than thirty seconds to play, the Heat are five points down. The situation seems hopeless; it appears that the championship is lost. In Miami, hundreds of spectators are streaming out of the arena.

That's how some so-called fans handle adversity: When things look bad for their team, they give up hope. They despair. They throw in the towel. And that — to put it bluntly — is just wrong. Because now — when the going gets tough — is no time to surrender to negativity and doubt. It is precisely at this time, at the darkest hour, when you need to reach deep down inside and — somehow, some way — find your inner strength. This is the time to *believe.*

This, in short, is a time for faith.

And at that moment, there in Israel, birthplace of religions, heartland of spirituality, I can *feel* something. That's right: Me, the nonbeliever, Mr. Cynical. I can *feel* it and I know it's real. I turn to Michelle and I tell her what I am feeling in my heart, my very *soul.*

"They're going to lose," I say.

But somehow, impossibly, they battle back. The arena is going insane. The Hebrew announcers are drenching their microphones in saliva. I am stalking around the room, shouting helpful advice to the Heat players. With five seconds left and the Heat trailing by three, Ray Allen, following my explicit instructions ("Make It! Make it! MAKEITMAKEITMAKEIT!"), hits a three-point shot that historians will someday rank, in terms of historical significance, alongside, if not just ahead of, the Louisiana Purchase. The Heat win in overtime, and cries of joy echo up and down the halls of the Kfar Blum Kibbutz Hotel.

So it's a pretty good morning.

After breakfast we board our bus and set out to see some more important ancient things that, to be brutally honest, we are not that excited about. If you've ever been on a longish bus tour, you know that at some point you just run out of gas. You cannot absorb another fascinating fact. But Doron still has plenty of pent-up information to impart to us and we don't want to let him down, so we file off the bus and trudge around, dutifully looking at and taking pictures of a series of mosaics, columns, random piles of stones, etc., left by the Greeks and Romans. At this point, we're wishing, as a tour group, that the Greeks and Romans had just stayed the hell back in Greece and Rome instead of coming here and littering the landscape with all these freaking *ruins.*

The low point comes when our tour takes us through yet *another* ancient water tunnel. Our feeling, as a tour group, is that if you have sloshed through one dark cramped clammy tunnel full of ancient water that you do not really know the source of, you have sloshed through them all. Nobody wants to do this one. But we do it. Because, dammit, we're *tourists.*

From the tunnel we proceed to Caesarea, an ancient Mediterranean port city, where we view, among other things, the ruins of a Roman latrine. Caesarea also has wifi, but that was installed after the Romans.

We end the day back where we started our Israel trip, in Tel Aviv. We have dinner at a dockside restaurant with Chicago mayor Rahm Emanuel. (Not in the sense of eating at the same table with him, but in the sense of seeing him walk past the restaurant while we're eating.) (At least we think it's him.)

Our time in Israel is almost done, and together our group has experienced many interesting, even amazing, things. Along the way we've been transformed from a semi-random collection of people who happened to be on a tour bus together into genuine friends. So it's not surprising that much of the conversation at dinner concerns Ray Allen.

DAY ELEVEN

We leave Israel today, so much of the day is spent preparing for the trip home, by which I of course mean: shopping. We also pack. I decide to throw out my defective forty-shekels-apiece sandals, which are pretty funky from sloshing through ancient historic underground water. My hope, as I put them into the hotel-room wastebasket, is that they will wind up in the hands of some less fortunate person, who will burn them.

We have our final group dinner, drinking toasts to Rabbi Eddie and Doron. Then it's back on the bus one last time for the trip to the airport and a bunch of good-bye hugs. Then we're on the overnight El Al flight back to the States. We land early in the morning; when we turn on our phones, we learn that the Miami Heat have won Game 7 and the NBA championship. I'm beginning to believe that there might be a Higher Power after all. Here I am referring to Le-Bron James.

So our Israel adventure ends on a happy note. Which is fitting because it was a great trip. Israel is a fascinating, beautiful place, and surprisingly welcoming. We'd been told that Israelis can be brusque, but almost everyone we encountered was helpful and friendly. The wifi is abundant and the food is excellent; the falafel should win some kind of Nobel Prize. We never felt unsafe, except the times when we were walking backward off the cliff and riding Thunderbolt the Racing Camel, both of which were our own fault.

Would we go back to Israel? We would in a heartbeat. In fact, we've already decided that we will and the reason is simple: Apparently we need more menorahs.

■ ■ ■ ■

How to Become a
Professional
Author

■ ■ ■ ■

Being a professional author is a great job. You get to work at home, be your own boss and wear whatever you want.

FACT: Ernest Hemingway wrote *The Sun Also Rises* wearing a penguin costume.*

Another benefit of being a professional author is you also have complete freedom to snack. I eat as many as forty-five distinct snacks per day. My typical schedule is, I spend several minutes working on writing something (this sentence, for example) and then I'll think to myself, quote, *"Snack time!"* Then I'll head to the kitchen to see what's available. There is basically nothing in my kitchen that I have not, at one time or another, as a professional author, smeared peanut butter on. I include pot holders in that statement.

And then there is the pay. It is excellent.

* And it was not a male penguin.

207

I'm not saying that you will, right off the bat, with no author experience, make the kind of money Stephen King makes. Achieving that level of success can take, literally, months. But the potential is there, especially if you are a fast typist, because the standard practice in the writing industry is to pay authors by the word. Let me repeat that statement for emphasis: The standard practice in the industry is to pay authors *by the word.* At this point, you are thinking to yourself in your mind: *Wait a minute, is he saying that the standard practice in the industry is to pay authors by the word?* Yes! That is what I am saying! (Specifically, I am saying that the standard practice in the industry is to pay authors by the word.)

Another thought you may have is: *Do I have what it takes to make the grade as a professional writer?* I will answer that question with brutal and unflinching honesty: Yes. Don't be discouraged if you have no formal training in the field of writing. Writing is not one of those activities that require a specific skill, such as golf, opera or radiator repair. You *can* be a writer. *Anyone* can be a writer.

FACT: William Shakespeare, who is responsible for some of the greatest works of Western literature including the original version of *West Side Story,* was raised in a rural village without any formal education and could neither read nor write nor speak English. Many historians now believe he may actually have been a horse.

FACT: When J. K. Rowling wrote the first Harry Potter book, she was a single mother on welfare who was both blind and deaf and had been chained to a dungeon wall for eleven years *upside down.*

FACT: John Grisham is from Mississippi.

If these individuals were able to overcome such hardships and become successful authors, there is no reason why you can't. So let's get started!

The first step is to have a snack.

(*Thirty-minute break.*)

OK, time to get started!

HOW TO BREAK INTO
THE WRITING FIELD

Let's get one thing straight: There are no shortcuts to becoming a successful published author. It takes determination and a lot of plain old hard work. You cannot just sit around and wait for literary success to be dropped on you out of the sky by some magical success-pooping seagull. No, you must roll up your sleeves, plant yourself in front of your computer and perform the difficult — and lonely — task of writing a letter to a successful author asking for free advice. This is the only known way to succeed as a writer. We published authors receive such letters all the time. Mine generally sound like this:

Dear Mr. Berry,

I am a recent college graduate or stay-at-home mother of three or corporate attorney or eighty-seven-year-old retiree or prison inmate or vice president of the United States and I am a big fan of your writing, especially your book "Hoot," which was hilarious! Anyway, the reason for this letter is that I am looking for some guidance and I am hoping you can provide it. While not a published author myself, I have done some writing in my spare time, and my friends or parents or college professors or cell mates or goldfish or alien abductors have told me that my "tongue in cheek" style of humor reminds them of you. Mr. Barrie, I know you are a very busy person so I will "cut to the chase." I am hoping you will take a look at the enclosed selection of my humorous essays or the 873-page manuscript of my comic novel about a corporate attorney who becomes involved in a series of wacky depositions or my collection of family Christmas newsletters from 1987 or the Akron, Ohio, Yellow Pages or my handwritten account of the many humorous events that occurred during my forty-three-year career in the field of dental implants. I am specifically wondering if you think that I have "what it takes" to "make the grade" as a "pro" writer and, if so, what steps I should take next? Would you be interested in "polishing up" my work for publication? I would of course give you "full credit." Also would it be possible for you to put in a "good word" for me with your publisher? I understand that in order to get published, it's a good idea to have an agent and I am hoping you can recommend one. I would also be grateful for any "tricks of the trade" you can pass along to a "rookie," such as the "do's and don'ts" of putting words inside "quotation marks." Also I have developed this weird lump on my right elbow and I'm wondering if you think I should have it looked at. Thank you so much, Mr. Berrie!

Sincerely,
(Name)

P.S. Please write back soon because the lump is changing color.

We professional authors receive many letters like this. Whenever one arrives, we immediately drop whatever we are doing so we can analyze the letter writer's specific situation and develop a detailed plan of action for his or her writing career. Bear in mind that this takes time. If you write to one of the more popular authors — James Patterson, for example, or the late Jane Austen — you need to be patient, as they might be busy providing consultation services for other aspiring authors. Allow two weeks for your author to get back to you. After that, you should consider a follow-up letter or personal visit to your author's residence to see how your career plan is coming along.

Your First Book Contract

Once your author has found you an agent and a publisher, you will need to sign a book contract, which is a lengthy legal document that says, "The Author warrants blah-blah-blah, etc." Don't worry about the exact contents of the contract. The only important thing in there is the size of your advance, which is a sum of money that the publisher pays you before you have actually written the book. That's right: You get this money *up front.* I realize this sounds crazy. It's like taking a college course where the professor gives you an "A" on a paper you haven't even written yet. But there's a sound logical reason for this system; namely, the book publishing industry has no idea what it's doing.

The size of your first advance will depend on a great many factors. It should be around one million dollars.

Writing a Book

At some point during the decade after you sign the contract the publisher is going to start asking you whiny questions about when you expect to finish your book. "In your contract," your publisher will say, "you specifically warranted that blah-blah-blah." As if you, a busy professional author, are supposed to remember *every single thing* you sign!

But the point is, there may come a time when you have to physically write a book. This is the worst part of being a professional author because you have to sit around thinking up words for days on end, which is unbelievably boring. After you become more established, you can skip this pesky chore

213

by doing what many top authors do; namely, think up book *ideas* but hire cheap foreign labor to write the actual books. If you go that route, make sure you read your book before you pass it along to the publisher because many foreign laborers don't have a strong grasp of English and sometimes they will totally screw up your idea.

FACT: *The Hunger Games,* as originally conceived by the author, was supposed to be a three-book series on the historical impact of salad dressing.

But, as a rule, your publisher will expect you to write your first book all by yourself. This means you will have to choose a genre. For your first effort, I recommend that you write a children's book. This genre has a couple of advantages. For one thing, you're writing for children and children are, let's face it, not the sharpest quills on the porcupine. You can write pretty much any idiot thing you want and they'll be fine with it. Also, children's books are typically just twenty-four pages long and consist almost entirely of large illustrations, so the total number of words you have to write is about the same as a standard grocery list.

FACT: The average children's book author works two hours per year.

The one important rule of children's

books is that they have to teach an Important Lesson. Here's the basic format:

Merle Moth Does a Big Thing

Page 1: Merle Moth loved to eat.

Page 2: Eat! Eat! Eat!

Page 3: Merle ate socks.

Page 4: Merle ate coats.

Page 5: Merle even ate hats!

Page 6: One day, Merle saw a blue shirt.

Page 7: "I will eat this shirt!" he said.

Page 8: But Merle could not eat the shirt.

Page 9: "This shirt tastes bad!" Merle told his friends.

Page 10: "Because it is made from oil," said Tyrone Toad.

Page 11: "What is oil?" said Merle.

Page 12: "It is a nonrenewable resource,"

said Earlene the Endangered Fruit Bat.

Page 13: "Oh no!" said Merle.

Page 14: "Oil hurts the Earth," said Carlos Cicada, who was transgendered.

Page 15: "Oh no!" said Merle again, for he knew the book needed to reach twenty-four pages.

Page 16: "Yes," said Reggie the Lactose-Intolerant Raccoon. "We must save the Earth from oil!"

Page 17: "But I am so small!" said Merle. "How can I save the Earth from oil?"

Page 18: "I know!" said Farook the Differently Abled Muslim Sea Urchin. "You can fly deep into the ear canal of a petrochemical executive and tell him to stop hurting the Earth with oil!"

Page 19: And that is what Merle did.

Page 20: Soon the Earth was saved!

Page 21: Merle was happy.

Page 22: "I learned an Important Lesson," he said. "Even if you are small, you can make a big difference!"

Page 23: "You can say that again!" said Antoine, a vegan amoeba of color.

Page 24: Everyone laughed and laughed. But not at anyone else.

The End

The downside to the children's book genre is that — this is well known inside the publishing industry — it's impossible to keep cranking out this kind of crap without turning to hard drugs.

FACT: *The Very Hungry Caterpillar* is actually about the author's long, desperate struggle with crystal meth.

For this reason you might want to consider another low-workload, high-pay genre: poetry. There is BIG money to be made here because poetry is extremely popular with the American consumer. Bookstores literally cannot keep poetry books on the shelves. (This is why, when you go to a bookstore, you never see poetry books on the shelves.)

"Wait a minute," I hear you saying. "Isn't

it hard to write a poem?"

It used to be. In the old days, there were strict rules requiring that poems had to rhyme and contain a certain number of syllables per line and be at least vaguely comprehensible to humans. Writing these old-style poems was backbreaking work, which is why the men who did it are virtually all dead today from various causes.

But then in the early nineteenth or twentieth century a group of brilliant young research poets working late at the National Poetry Laboratory accidentally mainlined some heroin and invented "free verse," which is a kind of poetry that has no rules at all. Now any random clot of unpunctuated words could be a poem:

Suddenly

In the morning
always in the morning
the moment comes
when you are shuffling, sleep-slowed
down the dawn-dim hallway
shuffling in your nightdress
it comes
so sudden
so cold
so suddenly cold when it comes

the dog nose in your butt.

— T. S. ELIOT

Free verse totally revolutionized the poetry industry. It meant that the entire lifetime output of an old-style poet such as Milton Wordsworth Longfellow could be equaled in a single afternoon by a bored homemaker with a bottle of zinfandel. The point is: *You can definitely do it.* And because of the high consumer demand for poetry, the money is *great.*

FACT: Eighty-six percent of all private jets are owned by poets.

Also it goes without saying that, as a poet, you will be a major international celebrity. You will have front-row seats for every concert and be whisked past the line of loser normal people into any exclusive restaurant or nightclub you want. Not to mention having casual sex with as many as four Kardashians *per day.*

If that sounds too unhygienic, you might want to consider becoming a novelist. This is a little harder than writing poetry or children's books, but not much. The two big decisions you have to make are:

Will it be a women's novel or a men's novel?

Will there be vampires?

219

Once you have answered these questions, all you have to do is come up with characters and a plot that contains a Beginning, a Middle and a Surprise Ending. Use this table for reference:

Elements of a Novel*

Women's Novel

MAIN CHARACTER
- Female. Strikingly beautiful. Highly intelligent. Sensitive. Has many feelings. Millions and millions of feelings. Very attractive to men. Also very attractive to women. Also very attractive to vampires if there are any in the plot. Just generally an extremely attractive person.

OTHER PRINCIPAL CHARACTERS
- The main character's mother or sister or daughter or childhood friend from whom she has become estranged or has an ambivalent relationship.
- Other females whose function is to have long conversations with the main character about her numerous feelings

* Source: Chaucer.

and relationship complexities.

- Several strikingly handsome males and/or vampires who are, it goes without saying, powerfully attracted to the main character.

BEGINNING

- We are gradually introduced to the world of the main character. We slowly begin to understand, through her innermost thoughts and her conversations with other female characters, that, because of some mysterious traumatic incident that occurred in the past, she has deeply conflicted feelings about her complex relationships with her mother, sister, daughter and/or estranged childhood friend. We also are introduced to one or more males to whom the main character is attracted but about whom she has many deeply ambivalent feelings that result in much conflicted thinking going on for pages and pages.

MIDDLE

- Through continued conversations with other female characters, as well as additional lengthy passages of innermost thoughts, we gradually learn more about the complex feelings and relationships of the main character, getting glimpses — but only glimpses — of the mysterious traumatic past incident that is causing her to have so much emotional complexity in her life. At the same time she gradually becomes involved in a deeper and more complex relationship with one or more of the male characters, yet she is unable to commit herself fully to him or them because of so many sensitive innermost ambivalent feelings swarming around inside her like minnows in a bait bucket.

SURPRISE ENDING

- As the main character's feelings reach a raging fever pitch of ambivalence, she has a climactic emotional conversation or encounter involving her mother, sister, daughter or estranged childhood friend, and we finally, after many hundreds of pages, discover the mysterious traumatic past event has caused so much internal conflict and relationship complexity. It turns out to be: a shocking surprise. By finally getting it out into the open, the main character is able to confront it and have many additional pages of conversations and thoughts and feelings about it. In the end she is able, at last, to accept herself as the highly attractive woman she is and to admit the love she feels for one or more of the male characters and possibly allow him to suck out her blood. The book ends here because of the danger that some actual action is about to occur.

Men's Novel

MAIN CHARACTER
- Male. Masculine. Ruggedly handsome. Brave. Manly. Highly intelligent. Fearless. A renegade and a loner; dislikes authority. Courageous. Strong and very good at fighting, but reluctant to use violence. Understood to possess — although this is never explicitly stated — a huge penis.

OTHER PRINCIPAL CHARACTERS
- A serial killer or sex pervert basement torturer or powerful politician or businessperson or criminal with numerous henchpersons.
- High-ranking yet idiotic police, military or government officials who detest

223

renegade loners.

- A highly professional yet beautiful female police or military officer or lawyer with a tough outer shell yet at the same time a certain emotional vulnerability yet at the same time a nice pair of gazombas.

BEGINNING

- The main character is thrust into a situation where he encounters some wrongdoing being done and, through no fault of his own, must reluctantly beat the living shit out of some hench-persons. This results in a string of mysterious clues that cause the main character to realize that there is an evil plot afoot involving worldwide nuclear destruction or serial killing or sex pervert basement torturing with soldering irons or the president of the United States being a Communist robot or some other hideous evil plot that the main character must courageously try to uncover single-handedly against impossible odds.

MIDDLE

- The main character, bravely pursuing the truth, finds his path blocked time and again by henchpersons out of whom he has no choice but to reluctantly beat the living shit. This draws the attention of high-ranking police, military or government officials who naturally get everything completely wrong and focus their suspicions on the main character. They assign, to investigate him, the tough yet beautiful gazomba woman. She and the main character take an instant dislike to each other and soon have amazing sex lasting several days thanks to the awesome power of the unstated but clearly understood Yule log in his undershorts.

SURPRISE ENDING

- The main character and the woman (who has of course fallen in love with him) become ensnared in a hopeless plot predicament from which escape is absolutely, completely one hundred percent impossible, so they are definitely going to die. They respond by having sex of a caliber that would kill a rhinoceros. Then they escape in a very clever and brave way and proceed to an action-packed climax in which the main character, against impossible odds, reluctantly kills a minimum of

135 people en route to discovering the incredible shocking truth, which is: something totally unexpected. With the plot now resolved, the main character and the woman again engage in love-making so powerful that it alters world-wide bird migration patterns, although she knows in her heart that he will never settle down with one woman because of his renegade loner lifestyle and massive unstated pelvic salami.

Promoting Your Book

The surest way to make your book a best-seller is to get my wife to read it. If she likes it, she *will* make it a bestseller. She has done this repeatedly. Remember a book called *The Kite Runner*? That was my wife. Of the ten million copies of that book sold, at least 9.8 million were purchased by people who were directly ordered to do so by my wife. Not only did she make everybody in her vast international network of book-reading women friends buy it, she also would walk up to complete strangers in bookstores and say: "Have you read *The Kite Runner*? It's a *great* book!" Then she would basically hover around them until they had no choice but to buy *The Kite Runner,* even if they already owned it or, for that matter, even if they owned the bookstore.

Remember the US Airways flight that hero pilot Chesley Sullenberger landed in the Hudson River after both engines died, and the passengers all miraculously survived? If my wife had been on the flight, when she and the other passengers were standing on the plane wings waiting for the rescue boats, she would have taken the opportunity to tell them that they needed to buy *The Kite Runner*.

Other books that my wife has, by relentlessly hectoring innocent bystanders, personally turned into bestsellers include *The Bridges of Madison County, Room* and *The Language of Flowers*.

Now to answer your questions:

- No, my wife has never made any of *my* books into bestsellers.

- Yes, I am her husband.

- Unlike, say, the author of *The Kite Runner*.

- No, I am not bitter.

- Really! I'm fine with it!

- Shut up.

But you cannot rely entirely on my wife to promote your book for you. You will also have to do some promoting yourself. One effective technique, especially for first-time authors, is to march into bookstores and inform the staff, in a loud yet irritated voice, that they don't have enough copies of your book, and don't have it displayed prominently enough, and clearly are not doing an adequate job of informing customers about it. Bookstore employees really appreciate receiving this kind of helpful input from authors and will definitely pay special attention to your books after you leave.

The Book Tour

As a bestselling author, you will be sent out on a book tour, which is a multi-city trip starting out in New York City and ending in death.

Ha-ha! I'm exaggerating of course.

FACT: Only eight percent of book tours are fatal to the author.

Nevertheless, book tours can be grueling because you go from city to city appearing on TV and radio shows where you will be interviewed by perky on-air personalities who have not read your book and sincerely do not give a shit about it. If they were interested in books, they would never have gotten into radio or TV in the first place. So it's up to you, the author, to "carry the ball" during these interviews, and it can be hard work, as we see in this classic author-interview transcript from the early days of radio:

Host: Our next guest is Herman Melville, who has written a book called *Moby-Duck*.

Melville: *Dick.*

Host: I beg your pardon?

Melville: It's *Dick*.

Host: What is?

Melville: The book title. It's *Moby-Dick*.

Host: *Dick?*

Melville: Yes. It's the name of a whale, which is a major character in the book.

Host: So this *Dick* is a talking whale?

Melville: No, the whale is essentially a symbol — of fate, of chaos, of uncertainty, of the vast uncontrollable and unknowable forces of the universe, against which man is powerless.

Host: I see. (*Pause.*) So there's no duck?

So book tours are not easy. But you still

should do them because there is no better way to "get the word out" about your book than to appear on TV, especially a major national show such as *The Daily Show with Jon Stewart, The Ellen DeGeneres Show, Dancing with the Stars* or *Mad Men.* You should go on as many of these shows as your schedule allows.

How to Get on a Major Television Show

It's extremely easy. These shows always need guests and they're especially eager to have authors who are promoting books. So you don't need an appointment or anything. Simply show up at the TV studio about fifteen minutes before the show starts and let the security people know you are available to be a guest. They will take it from there.

I myself have used this technique countless times to get on national TV shows. Here's a photograph of me taken on the set of the *Today Show,* where I am attempting to explain my book to four TV personalities who — this is clear from their expressions — have no idea who I am or what the hell I am doing there:

Getting Book Blurbs from Famous Authors

Blurbs are quotes printed on book jackets in which famous authors reveal their honest critical opinions of the book:

- *"It was OK for the first twenty pages, which was as far as I got."*

- *"Pretty much all I know about this book is that it's rectangular."*

- *"My agent, who's also the agent for the*

231

author of this book, asked me to write a blurb, so here's your fucking blurb."

I am of course kidding. Authors write blurbs because they have been pressured to do so by other authors or publishers or agents; they are never even remotely critical. No matter how crappy a book is, the blurbs always declare that it is not only a brilliant work of literature but it can also, if applied directly to the affected area, cure cancer.

Naturally you want your book to have blurbs from big-time authors. But how do you get them if you're just starting out and you don't *know* any big-time authors? The answer is — and here I am quoting directly from an official statement of the American Academy of Famous American Authors — "Lie."

That's right: These authors are officially granting you permission to go ahead and make up blurbs and claim they wrote them. They don't care anymore. They're sick and tired of being pestered to read books and then write ludicrously gushing praise that nobody with the IQ of a midrange hamster takes seriously anyway.

Improving Your Book's Amazon Ranking

Your book, along with millions of others, will be listed on the Amazon.com website, which will also show your book's sales ranking. As a professional author, you need to check this ranking a minimum of two hundred times per day so you can monitor exactly how your book is doing and respond accordingly.

For example, let's say you check Amazon at 6:23 a.m. and notice that your ranking is 2,325,217. That is, frankly, not a great ranking. So you boldly take action in the form of calling your mom and asking her to go on Amazon and purchase one or more copies of your book. If — and this can happen to you, as a professional author — your mom is no longer accepting your phone calls, you may have to purchase a copy of your book yourself.

Then you go back to checking Amazon every several minutes until finally, at 3:47 p.m., the rankings are updated and, *BOOM*, there's your book, sitting pretty, at number 2,304,958. That's right: Thanks to your decisive action, your book has moved up *more than 20,000 places*!

But you cannot rest on those laurels. You need to immediately resume checking Amazon because there are thousands and thousands of competing authors out there and we are all vigilantly monitoring our own rankings. It's our second-favorite activity, behind snacking. If you want to "stay in the race," you must do whatever is necessary to protect your book's ranking.

FACT: When J. R. R. Tolkien died, the police found seventeen million copies of *The Hobbit* in his garage.

Another helpful thing you can do is monitor the Amazon customer reviews and threaten to kill anybody who gives your book fewer than four stars. Joyce Carol Oates is famous for this.

Conclusion

So there you have it: The "inside story" on how to become a top professional author. These are proven techniques that *will work for you.* But don't just take my word for it: Take the word of Dan Brown, James Patterson, Dean Koontz, Patricia Cornwell, Robert Ludlum, the *Fifty Shades of Grey* woman, Jackie Collins, Dr. Seuss, Agatha Christie, Leo Tolstoy and Jay Z, all of whom have read this chapter and, speaking in unison, declared it to be "without question the most helpful thing ever written by anybody."

So now you have all the tools you need to

be a professional author. Now it's up to you. Follow your dream, do not give up and never, ever, let *anything* stand in your way.

It's time for another snack.

ABOUT THE AUTHOR

Dave Barry has written more than 30 books, including the novels *Big Trouble, Lunatics, Tricky Business* and, most recently, *Insane City*. He has also written several nonfiction works including *I'll Mature When I'm Dead*. Two of Barry's books were the basis for the CBS sitcom Dave's World. Barry lives in Miami with his family.